Regroup
THE HOW-TO OF
NEVER GIVING UP

JAUNIQUE SEALEY

INKSPIRATION PRESS
LOS ANGELES

REGROUP: THE HOW-TO OF NEVER GIVING UP

An Inkspiration Press Book
Published by Inkspiration Press (Los Angeles)

www.RegroupNation.com
www.Jaunique.com
www.InkspirationPress.com

The author is available for speaking engagements. For more information or to book an event, please use the contact form at www.Jaunique.com.

First Edition: April 2017
Library of Congress Control Number: 2017902119

ISBN 978-0-9817922-5-5 (Paperback)
ISBN 978-0-9817922-6-2 (eBook)
ISBN 978-0-9817922-7-9 (Audiobook)

Book Cover Design by: Christopher Pana
Interior Design by: Jaunique Sealey www.Jaunique.com
Author photo by: Frederic Charpentier, www.FredericPhotography.com
Interior lightbulb icon incorporated under license from Mikhail Firsov © 123RF.com

Manufactured in the United States of America.

For You

Contents

THE REGROUP

REFRAME

REFOCUS

REGROUP NATION

Author's Preface

I've written this book to give you an entirely different perspective on success. I am successful; but that alone doesn't make me *different*. Most successful people can tell you what they *think* made them successful, but really, they don't know and they have even less of an idea of whether or not it will work for you.

No one *along the way* to success thinks about making a map for others – they're too focused on the end goal to leave a trail of breadcrumbs for the competition. This is where I am *different*. Most of the things that I do are for the learning experience. Thankfully, in the process, I've done well, even without a specific focus on money. At some point, I decided that I wanted to learn what made success, well, success. Coming from a legacy of teachers, I believe that you haven't really learned something unless you could explain it to a 5 year old. That's been my standard for learning that got me to Duke (graduating high school with enough credits to skip most of the freshman year pre-requisites), to Harvard Law and to passing two Bar Exams in two states, in one shot. So, that was the standard I set for this subject, to ensure that the correct approach is applied to a complicated topic, making the information that I present clear, direct, and actionable.

Learning how to *be* successful for me came from observing, recording and interpreting my navigation of the process of becoming successful and what comes alongside it. I actually left the breadcrumbs with the intention of marking the way. What success means to me, in short, is setting a fulfilling goal, pursuing that goal and navigating all of the expected and unexpected setbacks and obstacles along the way, without giving up. And that last part is the most important. Everyone can dream, and everyone does. Everyone can set a goal and most people do. Many people will actually get going, but the overwhelming majority will stop before they reach the goal. That's the missing knowledge— *how not to give up*.

I wouldn't just write about success with nothing to add other than a 200 page version of my resume. You can find me on LinkedIn for that. In order to earn 200+ pages of your time, I need to present a novel perspective. And so, to write about finding *your* success, I have written a book about *failure*.

Through this book, I hope to show you and others how to

talk about failure and how to learn from it. Experiencing failure doesn't make you a Failure. The process and experience of failure is nothing to fear, nothing to be ashamed of, and in fact should be celebrated and studied. Failure is valuable experience. Imagine how much more we could learn from each other if we shared and discussed our own. This is my small contribution to try to change the world for the better.

Let's do this.

Introduction

This book is *not* a victory lap. This book is a *map*. After experiencing success in bone fide adulthood, I realized that all along, I really hadn't known very much about it.

The funny thing is, I certainly thought I knew – I guess we all do, but I was *wrong*. Similar to many, I grew up with the conventional idea of what success meant. To me success looked like big homes, fast cars, expensive jewelry, private jets, shopping sprees, trips to Paris and Hawaii, and hobnobbing with other elite, successful people. From my point of view, to become successful meant perfectionism leading to a cornerstone career achievement, followed by a financial windfall. And, at least according to *Forbes*, this was all supposed to happen before 40. *I've* never seen their "50 Under 50" list. Have you?

I was perfectly positioned to follow that path. I excelled in a rigorous high-school, and only applied to one college, Duke University, my first choice. I was accepted. At Duke I chose a challenging major in the Engineering School and while there, I worked intensely to gain acceptance into Harvard Law School, again my first choice. At Harvard, I worked even more relentlessly and earned a coveted summer internship at a prestigious Wall Street law firm in my first year of school. In law school, a summer internship is called a summer associate position. This is the gateway to permanent employment, if you manage to get an offer at the end of your summer. These jobs were the proverbial "golden ticket." If you stayed 10 years, you were guaranteed to become a millionaire as an attorney with no new skill set required other than the ability to work hard and build endurance for long hours.

While most students, even at Harvard Law School, would have no certainty of employment until a successful performance during the summer after their *second* year of law school, at the end of that summer after my *first* year, atypically, I was offered permanent employment. And, while seemingly on a rocket ship trajectory to the letter of what I was *supposed* to do, I opted to make a wide turn, wrenching my story off the traditional route.

I knew I was expected to remain on the pre-established path toward success, and while I was entirely grateful for the opportunities before me, something inside screamed for more – I wanted a different life. Although I aspired to success and even the riches that followed, I wanted to craft my own path toward it, whatever that entailed. And so, just when I had gotten comfortable with a relatively certain future, I decided to chart a different course.

I acted on my desire to work in the music industry and took a job, for less than half of what I had been offered at the law firm, at a startup record label. At the end of law school, I gave up my coveted law firm position and became an official employee of a company with an uncertain future.

The good times were short-lived. Just one year after graduation, funding for the company I had chosen over conventional wisdom, ran dry. The experience I had exchanged for my "golden ticket" now meant that my paychecks came in varying amounts, yet my bills stayed the same. I was devastated, but I had to figure a way out of my situation. I didn't realize it, but this was my first experience with traumatic failure and I felt woefully unprepared. My life of dreams had turned into a nightmare. In a panic, I found a second job that would allow me to work as many hours as I could physically stand— I pushed myself to the limit to maximize overtime pay. I did it so that I could continue to pay my rent and afford my car until I figured out my next move. I did it because each hour that I worked felt like one more hour I could put between myself and complete defeat. I could do it because I knew, somehow, that this would give me the resources I needed to create the options that would then help me find my next step.

That first smacking failure set me off on an unscripted journey, where I experienced many other setbacks to follow. I decided to move to a new city, Los Angeles, where I would find a wider range of opportunities. It took me a year to find my footing, as I navigated the gamut of money issues, searching for a job, housing instability and more. As I had gone "off script" so to speak, as an attorney, it was tough finding someone who wanted to take a chance on me and my unusual resume. Everyone else in my position had worked at a law firm, which was the conventional hiring profile. Even more of a barrier, as an attorney, you have to take and pass a rigorous Bar Exam in order to obtain a license to work in each state where you plan to practice. Although I took the exam three days after setting foot in California, results take at least six months to receive. So, I had to try different avenues to earn a living. I took jobs that I never imagined would follow having a law degree, like tutoring French, and collecting student email addresses on the University of Southern California campus as a marketing rep.

To be honest, while stumbling my way through it all in the early days, whenever I hit a setback, I'd immediately feel like giving up. And, in the face of adversity and extremely challenging circumstances, I did give up on some of the options I had created. I stopped shopping my screenplay, I gave up on writing the blog that I launched, I stopped going to auditions – ending all of my most entrepreneurial pursuits because I felt uncomfortable and wanted to run back as quickly as I could to the safety of my traditional path that, by this time, I was starting to think I should never have given up in the first place.

I had been trained and conditioned to believe, through years of traditional preparation, that a failure, setback or negative outcome was unequivocally bad and an indication that the path that led to it should be immediately abandoned and avoided. It was a very simple logic, reinforced by decades of grades, of binary *pass* and *fail* experiences; of applications and acceptance and measurement against a pre-existing mark. So, as I'm sure you can imagine, here I was thinking I could dare to dream, and try something different than virtually 99% of my classmates and I got knocked down and kicked as my seeming "reward" for taking a risk.

Once I had ventured off the treaded path and into the woods of charting my own course, it felt like life started to fight me, hitting me with challenge after challenge after challenge. At the time, I didn't know that I was supposed to fight back. I didn't know that I was supposed to ball up my fists and keep going. I had to learn. And once I realized that I would never find the conventional path fulfilling, I did start learning how to make my own way on the route less traveled.

In the pages that follow, I'm going to teach you how to make your own way, even out of no way – for whatever you desire. It doesn't matter if you want to find the courage to move just slightly from the norm, to stand out a little more from the crowd of your competition, or, instead go full steam into charting your own course, this book is your how-to guide with advice you'll need to know. This is how to not give up.

Resilience – the New *Must-Have* Skill

Let's face it, I'm an adventurer. I've only told you very little about myself so far, but I'm sure we'd agree on that. So, when I realized that my nature wasn't aligned with my preparation or conditioning, I had to learn a new skillset – one that would allow me to reframe my thinking and not quit when the setbacks arose. I had to learn to reinterpret obstacles, and frame impossible tasks as just another problem to be solved, in order to continue my journey. I had to learn how to turn situations that called for a complete breakdown into a needed breakthrough.

After cutting my teeth on bucking convention by moving to LA and establishing myself, things eventually started to turn in my favor. Before I knew it, I had managed to land what I thought was my dream job at the world's largest record company. I tried my best to stay happy with that, as long as I could—I really did. Although, I knew in that role, I was back in the groove of another well-worn path to the top. Again came that familiar feeling, of suffocation, of the desire for change and the need to make a new way for myself. So, again, I ventured off – away from the comforts of convention to start another adventure.

Change is Hard

We'll get to more of my story later – but now, let's shift gears to talk about you and what you'd like out of this time we'll spend together. If you enjoy consistent comfort—if you want to hold onto any excuse to stay the same, and keep your life the way it is, then this is probably not the book for you. The words that follow were written purposefully to spark a transformation. They were crafted with intention to walk you through a clear and effective process for achieving your goals. Experience may have already taught you that change is hard, so you know that in order to create a positive difference in your life, you have to want it.

Change uproots the comforts of what we know and can control, yet it is necessary to grow and thrive, and certainly to attain the highest reaches of our imagination. Everyone doesn't have to want or need broad sweeping changes – adventure isn't the warmest cup of tea. Sometimes, it's just incremental, done to achieve more fulfillment, breathe new life into a stale idea, or even simply to have more life options. Perhaps, you want change because the stress of the familiar is overwhelming and you need to find a clearer focus and less distraction. You are choosing for yourself more productivity, a better lifestyle, to take bolder risks and maximize your potential.

The current course of action isn't working. Innovation is needed to move past stubborn obstacles to achieve unfulfilled dreams. In order to get what you want, you need to change something. And that something, or someone, I should say, is *you*. Change is the only path for those who for any variety of reasons need to *find a new way*. The new way means obstacles and uncertainty that may have ended your previous attempts. This time, you're not on your own. I'm here with you – and I've got the map. This time, you'll know how to Regroup.

This is Your Success Story

Some part of you may still wonder what success has to do with regrouping. I understand why. These days, every success story sounds like a Eureka! moment—as if success runs in the veins of only a few pre-determined people and shows up through some miraculous immediate breakthrough or public victory. We hear about success as if it is only discovered, rather than deliberately invented. Like any good teacher, I happen to believe in showing the work.

The real story of breakthrough comes from learning about what was broken through. But we don't talk about this. Not soon enough – not while it's happening. And so we miss the best part of the story – the portion we could actually learn from, benefit from and use.

Challenges deliver setbacks and failures. This we know for sure. Most successful people have integrated and ingrained their responses to adversity so deeply that they don't even notice it anymore. That's a real loss for the rest of us. To reach that level of success, the one thing that they must have mastered, is how to expertly navigate adversity and setbacks while still maintaining a relentless dedication to their goals. How wonderful would it be to be taught *that* skillset?

Unfortunately, in our society, failure is associated with shame, so it is hidden. By the time most successful people feel confident enough to share their story, they generally no longer remember the most instructional details of how they achieved success. Instead, what they can explain is pieced together from the sporadic memories of a travelled path. Their best advice is often summarized by clichéd platitudes and generalities with no real meaning like, "never give up." But what does this mean, to "never give up?" I took it upon myself to learn. After much research, one-on-one interviews, and reviewing key moments of my own life, I learned it means, in short, to Regroup.

To Regroup means that no matter what happens, you always see the light illuminating your next step. And you take it. It means that you honor your pain, discouragement and disappointment; but you don't let them own you. You not only face the day with gratitude, but the night as well. To Regroup means that you learn your lessons and mark your accomplishments. It means that you're not afraid to face reality and that "reality checks" fuel and amplify your dreams rather than dull and deaden them. It means that you need good people around you and equally that you recognize the need to be of service to others. To Regroup means that you do not give up, even when you decide to quit. Regrouping is the unstoppable alignment of your purpose and power in a forward direction. You have this within you and now is the time to access it.

You Are Not Alone

At any given moment, there are millions of us who need to Regroup. Based on my experience, I believe that the greatest glories of my life, and yours, have and will come along with the relentless pursuit of very worthwhile goals. What makes a goal worthwhile is personal. I have my reasons and you'll have your own. For many, worthwhile means going after the big wins: following through on your dream of a new career; advancing in your current career; starting a new business, or educational pursuit; reaching health or fitness goals; or starting a family. These are some of the pillars of life that determine our daily experience, how we feel each morning, what we do during the day, how we view ourselves, and how we're able to maximize our time. Other worthwhile goals may be to learn how to declutter, minimize stress, find more time to spend with family, or how to paint, write code or garden. You're the only person who knows what truly lights your fire from the inside.

Despite living in times of uncertainty, we live in a period of unprecedented opportunity. Anyone can truly do anything and become the person that her or his mind conceives. What if you could harness that same process and that same power to your own benefit? To do your own good? What if you could become who you dream of being? And what if you could do what you dream of doing? If you could do anything you wanted to do, what would it be?

Aside from my educational pursuits, I have had four distinct and significant desires. First, I wanted to work in the music industry. You already know part of that story – except how it ended. I wound up in my *dream job* as an executive for the largest record company in the world, crafting the business models for the new digital era of the music business. I left to work with team Lady Gaga, and ultimately, I was hired directly by Prince. Second, I wanted the freedom to control my time and my geography. Since 2011, I haven't worked out of an office, nor has anyone determined my location or schedule other than me. Third, I wanted to publish my own book and become a paid speaker and writer. In 2012, I travelled nearly 100,000 miles around the world for paid engagements following the publication of my third book. Fourth, I wanted to launch a cosmetics brand that would be on QVC. This story, I'll tell you in the pages that follow. Do I have other goals? Sure – they're developing every day. But, my scorecard is different. This journey is my success. It is knowing that I can pick any goal that I want, and execute the same process to accomplish and see it through. When I hit an obstacle? I simply Regroup and keep going. What some people measure in money, I measure in an account of a different nature. I make sure my internal tank is full, and that my light is always on. This is my success. What is it that you really, truly want to do?

Success is not built on success. It's built on failure. It's built on frustration. Sometimes it's built on catastrophe.
– Sumner Redstone

To Talk About Success, Talk About Failure

To help you find your path, we need to take a unique approach to thinking about success and living in our purpose. To talk about success and to learn how to Regroup, we are going to have to talk about failure. As Albert Einstein once said, *"Failure is success in progress."* Talking about failure is how we show the process of success.

The topic of failure is uncomfortable and often swept under the rug as something we acknowledge but don't really want to entertain. Most often, when we reference failure, we speak of it as a fixed circumstance. Something *is* a failure, or even worse and more inaccurate, *he* or *she* is a Failure. To add further insult to the injury of these moments, we take them and make them shameful, magnifying the pain and discouragement that follows, virtually ensuring that we never get the full benefit of others' experiences. The time has come to set the record straight. As long as you have the gift of this day, it is impossible for you to truly or permanently fail.

Your Lightbulb Moment

I chose the symbol of this book very carefully. First, for reasons I'll explain in a second, I felt like it was the embodiment of what it means to Regroup. Second, I wanted you to have something that you would see everywhere that would remind you of your journey, to be able to recognize the brilliance all around you, and the certainty of your success if you just keep going.

Since it is such a mundane part of our lives today, it's hard to conceptualize what a landmark invention the lightbulb was at first. This was back in the day when candles were all people had to keep them out of the dark. Electric light paved the way for the industrial revolution and the advancement of science and education. It allowed us to control our internal environments and truly and comfortably set our own clocks, rather than being governed by the schedule of the sun. The lightbulb was the key that unlocked our ability to control time and circumstances. It illuminates our way, even when the time for darkness has come, so that we may continue. And this is exactly what Regrouping is.

> *"Genius is one per cent inspiration, ninety-nine percent perspiration."*
>
> – Edison

The perception that failure is final is an illusion that does us a disservice. It makes us think that we have permission to move on, resignedly, without reconsideration. We're encouraged to interpret failure as meaning that something is just "not for us" and that we should look for greener pastures rather than search for water to nurture the very grass we're standing on. This is not the path to success and it's certainly not what Edison so beautifully described. Success relies not just on luck, but on the experience gained by trying, failing and *learning*.

Keeping Track

Somewhere along the way of my journey, when I noticed a pattern in my experience of goal setting and reaching those goals, I began to keep a journal. I recognized that my mindset at the end of a challenging process was very different from what it had been along the way, and especially at the beginning. In order to truly know what the process of never giving up looked like, I was going to have to keep a record of my thoughts and feelings - a real-time representation of my internal environment.

One day as I was looking back through the journal, it dawned on me that I had solidified my approach – not giving up had become ingrained in my actions and philosophy. I realized that this was an incredibly powerful process to have. I started looking more carefully through each entry in my journal. Had I missed something? I remembered many times *feeling* overwhelmed and I certainly remembered *wanting to quit*. But why didn't I? What allowed me to keep going through the compounding of soul-crushing defeats, arriving one after another?

Looking back over my words, what I saw was unexpected. In the language of my journal was reflected an identifiable pattern of feelings, thoughts and behavior that I exhibited in making my way from one setback to the next. Unconsciously, I was doing the same things, using the same process and toolkit over and over again. Not only had I unknowingly developed a consistent and repeatable process for dealing with failure and traumatic setbacks, for doing the "impossible," but now I had a record of it – a map, so to speak, that I could process for myself and then share with others.

Once I had fully internalized this discovery, I began to look to others for signs of a similar process, especially those well-known for their success – in the breadcrumbs and fragments of what they said in interviews, memoirs, videos and blog posts. Once you know what you're looking for, you'd be surprised how much can be found. And what I did find was that there was an interconnection of instruction – not in the form of advice, but in the actual details of their *story*. While these incredible success examples were giving the well-meaning platitudes of "never give up" advice, hidden in their own story was the real treasure of *how*.

And so here I introduce to you the concept of *Regroup* – what it means to be resilient through life's harshest obstacles, and to reach your own space of resolve and conviction. This is a place where you do not face setbacks with resignation, but instead perseverance, resilience and grit. This is a process to give you clear passage to follow your own worthwhile goal into the life of your dreams by taking the bite out of what stops most people along the way. Because success is an unavoidable, inevitable destination if you could just learn how to keep going. Discover for yourself what it means to find inspiration in your toughest times and most challenging of circumstances.

In doing this, you become a member of my beloved Regroup Nation, my dream of building a coalition of dreamers and doers, who through purpose and conviction, live out the fullest corners of their lives with accomplishment and meaning.

Join me on this journey.

Chapter 1:
Three Truths About Failure, Loss and Unintended Outcomes

Failing, Falling and Flying

I had never flown on a private plane before this trip, yet, similar to our flight to New York, on the flight back to Minneapolis, I was one of only three passengers, including *the* legendary artist, Prince. At the outset, I was so green about this mode of travel that I started to panic, believing that we were going to "miss our flight" because we had arrived at the airport so late. Instead, almost synchronized with the last person's feet reaching the top of the airstairs, the airplane door closed immediately behind us and we taxied down the runway for takeoff.

On the flight, we discussed preparations for the impending

Welcome to Chicago performances and corresponding events. Even though I was originally employed as a lawyer for Prince and his record label, I had taken on some business responsibilities along with managerial duties for some of his New Power Generation roster artists. One of my first responsibilities was to make sure that one of the artists would make her promotional rounds and otherwise have a successful performance to introduce her to the Chicago audience. Although we were landing in Minneapolis near midnight, our flight in the morning to Chicago was just hours away.

Leaving the airport, from the back of our SUV, Prince said to me, "I'd like to do a performance before Chicago."

I didn't turn to look at him, but based on the simplicity of the statement and the hour of night, I thought that he was being wistful, rather than delivering notice of a wish to be fulfilled.

"I know, it would have been nice if we could." I said.

He didn't say another word the rest of the ride. In the seat behind me, he sat silently facing forward, his eyes covered by his customary dark glasses and his lips simply closed. Thinking the conversation was complete, I turned my thoughts to the next day's responsibilities as the car continued to Paisley Park.

Arriving at Paisley, I just expected that we, the business team, would drop Prince off, settle any lingering details for the next day and head off to the "home away from home" hotel to steal what was left of the sleeping hours for the night. So, if you can imagine, I was simply shocked to walk into the Paisley soundstage area and see the band bustling about in the lobby. It wasn't unusual for them to still be there, rehearsing at all hours of night; what was unusual was that they were actually packing up. *Quitting early?* I thought. *The night before we leave for a big show?* And then, I saw the girls, popping into the generous bathroom to put on their makeup. *Putting on makeup...* I wondered. And, then it clicked. We weren't going to the hotel and neither was the band. There was going to be a show.

I remember next being in the car speeding into downtown Minneapolis, arriving at First Avenue, the location made famous as Prince's first performance of the incomparable classic *Purple Rain.* The significance of history was lost to me in that moment, however, because my mind was sent reeling by the unfolding of a complete 15-piece band performance that had suddenly materialized before me in real time – all from a simple utterance on the way from the airport 45 minutes prior, that I thought should be dismissed as impossible.

It was *happening.* As I sat in the back corner of the darkened club, next to Prince at a two-top high table, the band had taken the stage and it was only then with a look of mild amusement that he said his next words to me.

"So what do you think, Jaunique?"

Simultaneously, I wanted to sink into the floor and float up to the clouds. Yes, my ego had been bruised a bit and I felt foolish in front of my idol turned boss, but I had learned that day. While my mind was conceiving impossibility, "impossible" was already being accomplished by someone with a different perspective.

The next day, we continued to Chicago and I wish I could say I had left my blunders in downtown Minneapolis. I hadn't.

Following a listening party at the Chicago House of Blues, we were to embark on a grueling schedule of morning shows and PR rounds the next day starting at 4:30 am. I probably went to bed at 3 am. Thank God for the amazing showers at the Chicago Four Seasons, it was the only good part of that day.

Before 5 am, I had assembled eleven members of Prince's band, The NPG, to accompany our artist to a morning show performance, scheduled to air at the 6 am hour. With everyone accounted for, we boarded the Sprinter bus and headed to the station. When we arrived, we entered a soundstage with nothing but a piano. No drum kit, no guitar amps, not even microphones, nothing needed for the performance. Nothing, except an 11-piece band, and me feeling like an incompetent disaster.

I was mortified. I called our PR executive on the West Coast and in her sleepy voice, she insistently told me that the lack of instruments was my fault, and that "everybody knows" that you need to order backline to perform at a television station. Everybody but me. Evidently, there is no "I" in everybody, because *I. did. not. know. that.*

Unbelievably, I had to shepherd the entire *professional* band back onto the bus because we were going to have to cancel the performance. To say I was devastated would be like calling an amputation a paper cut. I was stunned – and humiliated. If I could, I would have evaporated into the wind, and blown off in a wisp of the brisk Chicago morning air.

In full triage mode on the phone with Prince's manager, she was able to scramble a backup set of instruments from the United Center to meet us at the next interview location in time to make our appointment. I will never forget the relief I felt when I heard the sweet sound of those horns starting the familiar opening bars of the performance song. A relief that washed over quickly and was replaced with dread – knowing that there would be hell to pay when Prince found out.

Still operating on no sleep, once we had made our a.m. rounds, I collapsed on my bed at the hotel, not even taking notice of the luxe surroundings. My mother and cousin had driven in from Detroit, and it was all I could do to respond to their questions. Not only was I exhausted, I was also personally spent. Every atom in my body felt like lead. Sure, perhaps it was a rookie mistake, but the stakes were so high – on all levels. Eleven people dragged themselves out of their beds at the crack of dawn, for a broadcast television performance that had to be cancelled specifically because of *my* mistake. I had let myself down, our artist and the band, and worst of all, Prince, who had entrusted me with such a huge responsibility.

The tortuous minutes passed until the phone in my hotel room finally rang. The message was simple, "Your services are no longer needed here."

And just like that, the travel team called me to make my arrangements to take the first flight back to Los Angeles.

Once I got back to LA, I perched my shattered remains into a chair in my living room where I think I sat for days. I played it over in my mind, the incredible *Welcome to Chicago* performances at the United Center that I would be missing. How I was embarrassed and humiliated and disappointed and just, simply undone. For a week, I walked through my own echo chamber of thoughts – thinking I had not only completely blown my opportunity with Prince, but that I had also now become a Failure in the most spectacular way.

The pain was immense, an exquisite shame mixed with loss, mixed with a gripping and physical fear. It felt like a consequence that would alter the entire course of my life. As an engineer by education and an attorney by training, I had spent over a decade fully immersed in a world of precision and relentless attention to detail. I typically would never find myself in a completely unfamiliar circumstance, let alone over my head in a situation beyond my knowledge and capabilities. This was a first. My confidence was shaken - the very way I defined myself, as a competent professional, had been eroded. Sure, I had made mistakes in the past, but they had only been to my detriment, not others. I could make them invisible, socially and professionally as long as I internalized their effects, putting on a brave face to the world around me. But in this, my shame was public - my errors had touched others. I wondered how could I face them, any of them, ever again.

Now, perhaps the above seems a bit extreme – melodramatic, even. In retrospect, it was really not that big of a deal. Instruments were located, and the performance got rescheduled. I had been thrust into a completely unfamiliar situation; I made a rookie mistake – and we all lived to tell the tale. On the radar of life, this likely amounted to less than a blip. So why devote so much time to it?

At the time of a setback, of a failure or mishap, there is no perspective. There is only the present. And in the present, you feel overwhelmed, drowning in your own feelings and perhaps even the immediate judgments of others. Time has not yet addressed the chaos you feel within; you have no way of contextualizing the current events in light of their future resolution. The weight of *now* is the heaviest burden.

During one of my very first conversations with Prince, he told me the story of his friend, another well-known musician, who had cultivated a spirit of freedom and fearlessness in his daughter. A trait Prince seemed to admire. He said that he asked his friend what he did to give her that nature. In reply, the friend said that as a little girl, he would take his daughter to a flight of stairs. He'd put her on the step, lower ones at first, stand back a bit, and encourage her to jump into his arms. Of course, he caught her. Their game continued over time, progressing to higher and higher steps. Yet, no matter how high she climbed and how far the fall, her father always caught her. Of this, Prince said, "this is what I want for you." His "you" was generous and wasn't just in reference to me; it meant all of us working for him.

It took me a long time to understand, but I began to realize that I was fooling no one about my lack of experience as I attempted new things. He knew that I was a novice. I was the one who didn't know. He wasn't giving me opportunities to fail, he was giving me opportunities to *fly*.

About a week passed following my first class seat on the "flight of shame" back to Los Angeles. I was contemplating moving to Antarctica where I wouldn't have to tell anyone that I'd been fired by *the* Prince when my phone rang.

And just as if I hadn't been sent to my own planet of misery, as sure as if nothing had happened, Prince's manager was on the line with a new assignment.

"But...I thought I had been fired?" I managed to say.

"Oh, you were. From Chicago and working with his artist. Now, Prince wants you to only work with him."

You can't learn to fly without spreading your wings and taking leaps. My time with Prince was a first-hand education in many of the fundamental qualities of life: dedication to excellence, hard work, determination, resilience. But, what I really learned was that nothing in life, no matter how big the moment seems at the time, is important enough to stop you from trying again. You can always fix what is broken; you can always make your second chance, but you can never regain the chance you didn't take. I realized that impossible, really, is just your opinion. And sometimes in life, it just might take getting fired, to get promoted.

Talking About Failure

We simply do not talk enough about our failures. Especially the really painful, catastrophic ones that threaten our very sense of self. These are the failures that leave us vulnerable to the judgment of others. There's something about setback that feels so deeply personal, that if we do share it with someone, it's almost as if we've given a key to open the very core of who we are as a person. And perhaps, we won't have any protection for what is found there. Holding our failures in, and making them secrets makes us susceptible to the crushing weight of shame that we've been taught to associate with failure.

Even the word *failure* has its own power – it implies an inherent trait of character that once triggered, risks becoming an immutable, predictive and concrete description of its owner. It's as much of a weapon as it is a label, bludgeoning the accused with a hopeless future and summarily wiping away prior accomplishments.

Yet, when we speak of *success* – it too carries a meaning beyond its definition. Success is a badge of honor to be worn by its holder that may often even substitute for actual character failings. It is referred to as a result, a finality that also wipes away any semblance of *process*, especially the process that led to its achievement.

In the way we commonly speak, you *become* a Success or a Failure, rather than having *achieved* a success or having *experienced* a failure. And we subscribe to this perception, even though the latter is closer to reality. In fact, success and failure are impermanent, fleeting results – creations outside of the person, not the person herself.

When we hide our failures, we create the space for fear to foster. But *why*? Why be afraid to fail? If we knew more about what was on the other side of failure, how it can serve us and what makes it a part of success, we'd develop a power over this fear. For that to happen, however, we have to stop hiding our failures. We have to *talk* about them.

We race to hear stories of *success* but are only just starting to acknowledge in our collective consciousness that failure also deserves its seat at the table. Without the complete story of the role that failure plays, the biggest and most visible success stories become little more than victory laps, often coming up short in helping the rest of us understand the key question: *How did you survive that with your dream intact?*

Without the answer to that question – without the lesson and knowledge of an accessible process that we ourselves could repeat, we assign mythological status to the heroes of the success stories we know. We subscribe to this categorization of "us" and "them," choosing to increase the distance between ourselves and our own dreams, and accept the thinking that only certain people have the *stroke of luck*. But in true innovation, in creative pursuits and in living the life of one's dreams, there is no such thing as luck. There is only a process. Knowledge of this process can close the door to fear of failure and conquer the experience of disappointment and doubt that comes from ambitious pursuits.

When the Stakes are High

It's not the simple losses that sting—the loss of a regular season game, the loss of a dollar or a small bet in the casino. These are the easy "coin toss" failures that we can ignore. Not only have we risked and lost little, but we expected little as well.

Compare this to a situation in which you expected a result that would change the fundamental condition of your life in some way and possibly even risked something of similar value.

This is the loss and resulting disappointment that we're all afraid of. We run from it – because it is sure to be painful. We avoid it because we don't know the damage it will wreck against us. We don't know what it will take from us and if we will ever get it back. It is the proverbial monster under the bed, lying in wait for our tiniest slip up, to then drag us into the abyss.

These are the losses that feel most debilitating. Yet, as I learned, even when we encounter them, we can find a way to move on. Perhaps not without pain or hard work, but we can certainly survive it to meet the opportunity of another day.

Beyoncé and the Risk of the "This is It" Narrative

In 2013, without warning or promotion, international superstar Beyoncé released an eponymous "visual album" that reached platinum status almost overnight. Not only did she coin the term "visual album," her popularity also drove an innovation that changed the entire music industry and the way new albums are released. It is now normal to hear about an album release through friends first or via social media, as a "surprise release."

On that album, there is a song called "Flawless" that begins with footage of a young Beyoncé appearing on the television show *Star Search* along with her group Girls Tyme.[1] The segment is short, but if you watch a longer version, you'll see these young ladies stand perfectly still as their performance is rated, resulting in a disappointing loss to their competitor, a metal band named Skeleton Crew, that incidentally no one has heard from since.[2]

While exploring failure, these were the moments that in-trigued me. To more fully understand, I did some additional research.

Beyoncé knew that she wanted to be a singer and evinced tal-ent at an early age. To foster her gifts, her parents began entering her into talent competitions starting in the first grade. She won all of them, a reported 35 in a row, and soon outgrew the local opportunities available to her.[3] Shortly after, and as a result of her growing visibility, she became the anchoring member of a new girls group. Before it became Girls Tyme, it had gone through many iterations, with its 6 members performing under a variety of different names such as Something Fresh and Clyché.

The girls entertained around the Houston area, doing slick R&B-based song and dance routines for schools and talent shows, perfecting their act until in 1992, they made it to the finals of the celebrated instant-celebrity televised platform known at that time as Ed McMahon's *Star Search*. Speaking of the experi-ence, in her documentary art-piece "Self-Titled," Beyoncé says:

> *...I thought of this performance, which was a really defin-ing moment in my life as a child.... In my mind, we would perform on 'Star Search'—we would win. We would get a record deal and that was my dream at the time.*
>
> *No way in the world I would have ever imagined losing as a possibility. At the time I was only 9 years old, so at that*

time you don't realize that you could actually work super
hard and give everything you have, and lose. It was the
best message for me…The reality is, sometimes you lose. And
you're never too good to lose. And you're never too big to lose
and you're never too smart to lose. It happens. And you have
to embrace those things.[4]

I'm sure that many people heard those words and glossed over them. She put the experience in perfect perspective. A long time had passed since then. But usually, at the time it happens, a loss or failure in a supposed "all or nothing" moment is devastating and debilitating. It requires a special approach to come back from it and even more concerted effort to use the experience in service of your later goal. To read between the lines, and better understand what Beyoncé's experience could teach, I had to go back and get additional context for that Star Search experience to find the missing detail of what happened behind the scenes without the healing benefit of time and before the obvious resolution of the setback.

As Beyoncé said, she and her group believed that *Star Search* was going to be a one-way ticket to a record deal. That didn't happen. In her autobiography, *Soul Survivors*, written with members of the later-formed Destiny's Child, Beyoncé said of the moment immediately following the loss, "We all went crazy from crying. There was a lot riding on that performance."[5] Later, following the airing of the *Star Search* episode, the adults tried to put the failure in perspective, assuring the girls that they would indeed have their shot. They tried to lift their spirits and encourage the girls not to quit and to hold on to their dreams. Beyoncé says of the night that followed, "We cried ourselves to sleep that night...and we thought about what my parents had said. The next morning, we all woke up saying, 'Forget it. We don't have what it takes. We'll never get another shot at performing on TV...'"[6]

But soon after, the girls began watching the video recording of their performance. They watched it over and over again. And in watching it, they started to realize, they did not win because they did not deserve to win. It wasn't the best performance they could have given. In fact, with each viewing of the tape, they began to identify more and more errors that, if corrected, could have made a dramatic improvement. Not far beyond their reach or level of mastery, these were things that they already knew how to do. Says Beyoncé of this development:

> "*Each time [that we watched], our mistakes became more apparent. One girl's voice was off key. Another girl would forget a step. ...We needed some work. We were good for our age, but that's not good enough to make it in the real world. It's a good thing that we did not win any sympathy votes—otherwise we might not have worked so hard to get where we are today.*"

Adding to their important realization, Beyoncé's father, Matthew Knowles, informed the girls that *Star Search* producer Al

Masini told him that some artists that lose on the show went on to achieve tremendous musical success. Rather than the more general words previously at dinner, it was these carefully-researched and credible words that served to start to rebuild their confidence and sprits.

Next, Matthew Knowles, then a well-compensated salesman at IBM, quit his job in order to focus on training the girls for the real competition of earning a record deal along a more conventional path.[7] We've all heard of some of the arduous and grueling preparation, even at 11 years old, like running while in heels, and singing for 2 miles or more to build their performance endurance. They would subject themselves to seemingly endless rehearsals, a boot camp of constant preparation.

And circumstances got worse. While Matthew's career as an executive had afforded the family a large six-bedroom house in the toney Houston suburbs, the financial pressures of the focus on Beyoncé's career led to loss of the family home and ultimately a temporary split in the adult Knowles' marriage around Christmas time in 1994.[8]

The split was temporary, but the problems were not. It took two more auditions before Girls Tyme was signed to a major record label, Elektra Records. But, after just eight months, without a commercially successful album release, they received a letter letting them know that their contract would end. They were dropped. And again, it was devastating.

But this time, however, having survived not one, but two catastrophic failures, devastation turned into determination and they got better. To move forward in their purpose, they would need a new name. And it was here that Destiny's Child was formed. Continuing to perform and hone their skills, they were eventually given the opportunity to audition again, ironically in front of the same Columbia Records executive that had previously rejected them. This time, they were offered a record deal, their album was released and now, after having filled in the blanks of all of these facts, from here we can say the rest is history.

How many times have you gone into a big opportunity, whether it be a job interview, an audition, a meeting for a loan, or time with an important person that for one reason or another seems to hold the key to your future? Like Beyoncé with her *Star Search* moment, you've worked to a certain level and a huge opportunity appears that you think you're ready for, but it ends in disappointment. We spin ourselves into high expectations, encouraged by "instant success" stories portrayed by television shows like *Star Search*, and *American Idol*, and now *Shark Tank*. For the sake of building "must see" drama, we are encouraged to buy in to the myth of "it all boils down to this one moment." But, as you can see with Beyoncé's story, as long as you continue to work towards your purpose, nothing can be further from the truth.

I like this story in particular because it illustrates a common thought process mistake that we all have likely made when it comes to our dreams. Beyoncé's true dream was to be a star—not just a member of a group with a recording contract. But in her young mind, securing a recording contract was the way to becoming a star. So, the loss on *Star Search* was devastating. Thankfully, she kept at it. Destiny's Child secured a recording contract from Columbia and what followed this milestone, was the release of the debut Destiny's Child record and the beginnings of the stardom that Beyoncé originally had mistakenly pinned on a simple *Star Search* appearance. So, as she learned, not only did performing on *Star Search* not necessarily equate to getting a record deal, but getting a record deal didn't necessarily equate to becoming a star or having the success she truly dreamed of. Beyond this, after having experienced nothing but winning prior to her *Star Search* appearance, this seemed to be just the loss she needed to realize the next-level work required to truly accomplish her next-level goal.

When you're served a crushing defeat, in a supposed "all or nothing" moment, and things don't go well, it feels like the end of the world. It is the end of the world. Of *that* world. Of that set of circumstances—of that path to the future that you had so perfectly imagined going a certain way in your mind.

This is the roughest part—the feeling that it's all or nothing— one shot that makes or breaks you. This is a legend that we like to believe, but the reality is that it is far from the truth. Almost every great success story that I have ever heard starts with a failure of some sort.

Nothing Stopping You

There are many "all or nothing" moments that we create for ourselves in our lives. And because of the high expectations that we've created, and the extremes of what we're willing to risk to pursue them, we find ourselves on a well-trod path to disappointment and discouragement. Realistically, while we can learn to better control the expectations of high-stakes opportunities, we can also begin to understand how to prevent failure or the fear of failure from becoming a stopping point when things are not going as planned. There is no such thing as a "make-or –break" moment unless you let that moment break you. The key to success is to emerge unbroken, and this is entirely within your control.

Now, more than ever, success takes its shape in our lives as a process, rather than a destination. When you're able to see the work put in by others, it becomes that much easier to understand how to replicate a successful path for yourself, and as a result, to achieve your own dreams.

Success means moving past the setbacks with a continued focus on your goal. As you do more, you learn more. You earn the knowledge of new and better ways to accomplish objectives that are part of your journey. This allows you to apply those hard-won teachings to build an even greater understanding of your goal and what it actually will take to achieve it. Gradually, more and more of the process falls within your control, and once you get going, the momentum makes you unstoppable. At that point, the only thing that becomes impossible for you is giving up.

In the next chapter, I'll unpack what happens at the point of a setback – in your mind, and to your spirit. And I'll introduce the Regroup process.

THE REGROUP

Chapter 2:
Control Your Inner Dialogue

Wired to Conserve Energy

As humans, we have a propensity to conserve energy. Blame our biology. We're not inclined to expend effort on doing something, unless we can be reasonably assured of a likely payoff. This is quite bad news if you face the prospect of starting a new or innovative process, moving beyond a setback or disappointment, or if you perceive that the odds are stacked against you in some way or another.

A team of scientists at Simon Frasier University in Vancouver discovered that the human body, in search of even the smallest energy savings, will contort itself almost instantly to minimize caloric spend when walking. The researchers outfitted subjects with equipment that monitored the body's adjustment to gait while walking and in response to small adjustments delivered via knee-brace. When the experimental conditions made it more difficult to walk, the body naturally, and quickly made an assessment, then near-instantly maneuvered itself to continue the activity in the most calorie-efficient way. Evidently, our own nervous system performs this "optimization" in "real-time." Constantly making assessments and adjustments to keep us from wasting valuable energy.[9]

When calories were scarce, these kind of life-saving efficiencies would play an important role in ensuring our survival. Now, faced with different concerns and a deeper hunger for personal fulfillment and growth, this force of inertia creates an invisible barrier to our highest ambitions.

As members of modern society, it seems as though we've spent much of our efforts trying to push ourselves beyond our biological and psychological limits. We attempt to push beyond tribalism to build an ideal nation blended harmoniously between the lines of color, religion, sex and culture. At our best, we strive to excel beyond fear and ignorance, to chase the limits of knowledge and physical boundaries, conquering scientific theorems with breakthroughs as much as we conquer the heights of our tallest mountains and even go beyond the constraints of our atmosphere. We may have limits as humans, but we are winners in spirit— and we just keep pressing on, resisting any threatened force that would hold us back and defeat our progress.

But, given that the most basic, survival-function nature of your own biology is moving in its own way against you, once it is triggered, how can you triumph over it? How do you afford yourself the benefit of moving beyond a setback? And how do you avoid giving up even before you get started?

Knowing Your Enemy

By knowing and exploring the innate power of the forces that threaten us into the inertia of giving up, or even worse, never starting at all, we can build our internal ability to combat them. The first step to defeating your enemy, is knowing you have one. That means knowing that the impulse to harshly critique the benefits of your effort, and to overestimate the meaning of a negative result are hard-wired into our brains.

Understanding that force liberated me from it. I imagined the battle of wills that takes place after any setback. Our minds, in an attempt to protect our resources, are our harshest critics when considering which efforts would be a productive use of our energy. If the path forward is unknown, if there have been a few unsuccessful attempts, or—if someone else has found their way to doing it first (especially if we think we don't match up to the competition)—that mechanism springs to action and pushes us to draw a premature conclusion. Or, to parallel the Canadian study, once we've encountered an obstacle or any kind of indication that our current or intended efforts will not be successful, we're biologically pushed to draw a conclusion as soon as possible with the intent to stop ourselves from moving forward now and in the future.

To abandon your "fruitless'" efforts, from your body's perspective, is to conserve energy for not just some other unknown opportunity, but for *survival*. It's a false priority. Because of this, once we hit a setback or a sign of discouragement, our mind pushes us to stand still and hope for new grass on the horizon, rather than looking for water for the grass that we're currently standing on. Our mind, to avoid work, is constantly feeding a "grass is greener" scenario.

Let's Get Personal

Reading through the journal I used to record my thoughts and feelings during a particularly challenging three months, the "Season of Catastrophe" as I like to call it, I was surprised to find how shockingly pessimistic my thoughts were. To fully understand, it might be helpful to have some context…

Following my working experience with Prince, I returned to my agency and met an incredible mentor named Craig Bouchard through working with him on a charitable children's project, *The Adventures of Ai*. As part of our effort, we launched an international youth empowerment platform centered on an adventure novel and a mobile application of the same name that has reached the tops of the App Store charts in a number of countries outside of the US.

Following this, a new opportunity arose and I was asked to present a plan to reconceptualize and relaunch a cosmetics brand, named Cosmedicine. As a brand, it was like a cat, on its third life, the prior two being near-successes but eventually running out of money before any true stride was reached. In my go at it, we were determined to make it work, but as things inevitably happen with new companies, all does not always work out as planned.

Cosmedicine's particular advantage was its formulas. They were developed to be able to withstand rigorous clinical testing to evidence absolute results against the product claims. If you've ever used a beauty serum before, you'll know that that is a *big deal*. Speaking for my fellow beauty junkies, all that we want is to be able to buy something that is going to do what it promises. In forming Cosmedicine, the original team before me set out to differentiate the brand by making sure that the products offered would do just that – regardless of expense or difficulty in creating the formulas. The development and testing alone took 4 years.

When I came on board, this was exactly the type of history that I found interesting. Not only had I found the products that I had always wanted to use, but here was a brand with a story that was worthy of telling. Rather than spending a lot of money on advertising, we paid attention to refreshing our products and packaging. Our team buckled down and focused on going right to our customer and building a relationship of trust. It was re-freshing on both ends to be fully transparent because the quality was there and the intention was high.

At the outset, my plan was to build the brand via social and online media, and through direct-to-consumer sales, culminating eventually in a larger "official" launch on the QVC home shopping network. Our plan was unfolding slowly but surely. It is how in twelve months we amassed over 60,000 Facebook likes and monthly website traffic ranging from 12,000 to 20,000 visits, often resulting in three and nearly four-figure purchases of cosmetics by our incredible and loyal customer base.

Launching the brand on QVC had been a particular focused goal for the two years of planning plus one year of operations that led up to what would ultimately be our initial airdate on the channel in October 2016. After successfully tackling all of the challenges that this achievement required, what should have been an exciting time was complicated. Just as we received confirmation of our appearance on the network, I also learned that Cosmedicine the company was to be sold. And, if I couldn't find my own buyer to meet the deal terms of the required purchase price, it would be sold without me. That meant that me and the rest of my team would lose our jobs and everything that we had poured our hearts and souls into building for the business.

Although by this time, I had learned how not to give up, this set of circumstances would be the biggest challenge yet. Instead of experiencing the elation and joy of our impending QVC appearance, I was filled with worry and concern. I couldn't put my

full focus on that because I was saddled with the extremely difficult task of finding a buyer for a company that had just barely one
full year of operation. Normally, you need much more of a track
record. On top of this, I learned that I'd only have a small fraction
of the time that a deal like this would normally take.

It would be great if I could tell you that I blazed through all of
these hurdles like a rockstar. However, if I did, that doesn't make
for much of a story. And that is not what happened. Not at all. I
was stretched to capacity and had to hold on for dear life to the
chaotic ride that was unfolding. This was a true test of not giving
up. I'll tell you what did happen.

In spite of the background events at Cosmedicine's corporate
level, I still had to move forward with the QVC appearance. In
my mind, if we went on QVC and did well, especially if we sold
out of our product, we'd quickly find a willing buyer for the company, our deal would get done on time and all of our efforts with
Cosmedicine would be saved. Although my hopes were high, often the weight of the circumstances would get to me. In the days
leading up to QVC, in my journal, I wrote:

It's exhausting being on the sometimes hourly rollercoaster
of my moods – all at once travelling from the highs of elation to
the trough of despair and combating despondency, all depend-
ing on the narrative of my mind's interpretation of the facts at
hand. And while it doesn't seem fair – something that I want to
scream from the highest mountaintop until my vocal cords are

45

raw, it is still the reality with which I am coping, against which I continually try to hold my head up, unbowed by shame and faithlessness. My mind's chatter has really become crushing. The joy I imagine that I should be feeling at having our shot on QVC is replaced by pure trepidation and depression as I imagine that these circumstances could be unending and truly reflective of what my efforts have amounted to. I feel today, as if I am ruined.

When our airdate finally did come, the experience of QVC itself was overwhelming. I arrived at their expansive campus in West Chester, Pennsylvania, with perfect makeup, bouncing hair and a beautiful bright blue dress. I might have been scared, but at least I was going to look good, no matter what happened. From the time the earpiece was clipped underneath my hair and the microphone was attached to my dress—walking down the hallway to the soundstage, it was a blur. This was really going to happen. I passed through the double doors to brilliant lights and what seemed like a dozen massive camera rigs, that look in my memory's eye like giant brown grasshoppers. Voices directed at me echoed hollowly as I could barely process anything that I saw or heard. *This would be it.*

On set, I watched as the last 2 minutes of the segment prior to mine counted down to the unbelievable moment that our host Sandra would make the tease that Cosmedicine would be up next. I couldn't believe that I was watching her utter the words

"Cosmedicine" and "coming up next." Our model for the demonstration was asking me final questions about the specifics of how she was to apply our product on camera, but all I could do was mumble something incoherent as I tried to stay calm and focused. To be honest, I didn't want to speak to her or anyone for fear that the words I would need to say during our presentation were going to leave my mind.

All of a sudden, in a whoosh, it was a time to head into the view of the camera. Our beautiful pink and rose gold product was already delicately and elegantly arranged on the elevated display and it was go time. Sandra started and I tried to follow along. It seemed like time sped up and slowed down simultaneously. I was juggling trying to get out our story, following the right camera, demonstrating the product, giving information about it, speaking to the before and after images – figuring out what the people at home were watching and more.

All of a sudden, it was over. In a flash, just almost as if I walked in and walked out all at the same time, I was leaving. I left the soundstage and walked alone down the same fluorescent-lit hallway – my kitten heels echoing in clicks against the floor tiles.

When I waked into the green room, where people wait before and after their appearance time, I got the news. "It's not looking great." Our consultant told us as she turned from watching the monitors that showed the sales tallies. I needed to know what that meant, so I asked.

"Well, if they don't decide to give you a second airing, they'll ship all the inventory back to you and that's that. If that happens, all you can do is try to keep the door open—try to come back with another product—keep pushing."

It was like the description of doomsday. And suddenly, there I was again, back in that same binary world of pass and fail. Of failure and success. And to me, we had *failed*. *I had failed*. Not miserably, but certainly. It was not a win. And I was devastated. It was really all that I could do to manage the sudden rush of adrenaline that had been propping me up leave my body. But on top of that – this major moment, a major accomplishment in itself to result in such an incredible failure felt almost impossible to bear. I felt the crushing weight of disappointment and pessimistic despair compress me into feeling almost invisible. Optimism was too far to reach for. It was over, done. I had my shot, I took it for the team, and lost.

Once I had gotten back to my hotel room, the flood of congratulatory messages was overwhelming and made me feel worse. Now, beyond myself, here were more people that I let down. I had determined that having a fantastic result during this appearance was going to be the one way that we'd be able to secure a buyer for the company in the necessary timeframe. Now, it seemed like that wasn't going to happen, and worse, that we had closed the door to QVC forever.

After sitting on my bed for a bit to gather my thoughts, I let all the negative emotions come and pass. I took a deep breath and started to think about whether there was anything at all I could do now, rather than simply wait for bad news. I pulled out my laptop and started writing. I listed all of the things that in retrospect I wish that I had done differently. I wrote down my lessons learned and eventually I had enough of an analysis of my appearance that it started to look like a pretty good case for a second shot. I worked on it a bit more and then crafted it into an email to send to our buyer. After I hit send, knowing that I had nothing more I could do, I drifted off to sleep for my flight the next day.

Returning from the experience, we tried to make the most of the scenario before us, but given the circumstances, everything that went wrong was magnified in my own mind as an indictment of our future prospects to find a buyer. Following a slow day of sales, I wrote:

> I'm concerned. I'm concerned that the plans I have for it are not possible or that I don't have the wherewithal or the ideas to execute it. That this is all a fool's errand and perhaps my best efforts would be towards getting a job that could provide more certain income and stability in this time of uncertainty and destabilization. My mind has spiraled out of control. I admit it.

I share this deeply personal story with you, and the raw context from my journal because I think that this is the best way to show you the truth about what it means to Regroup, especially in facing difficult and heavy circumstances. It is important for you to see that not giving up doesn't mean that you don't feel like giving up, or think about giving up. It doesn't mean that you don't experience strong negative emotions or discouraging thoughts. They happen and at times can be overwhelming. I'm sharing mine because this is what a big failure looks and feels like in real time. I want to show you my thoughts and feelings so that you can start observing and building awareness of your own. From this place, we can start moving into how to make sure that a setback, no matter how big, doesn't turn into a stopping point.

Maybe You Can Relate

The pain of failure feels debilitating. It is a death of sorts. It's so much easier in a sense to give in to the internal narrative of defeat - that it's permanent. That it's too hard to overcome. As I wrote my unfettered thoughts, with efforts to do my best to completely capture the rawest truth of what I was feeling, in difficult times, "never" and "always" appeared quite often in my journal, as fatalistic assessments of the circumstances at hand, and "maybe you're not" appeared as defeatist self-judgments as well. Moreover, imagining what others might think or say, especially the naysayers, served to magnify the feelings of shame.

Most frightening about this type of disabling emotional experience was feeling like I had no power or control over it. Even though I had developed a mental comfort with failing, I still felt deeply afraid of being entirely overwhelmed. I was afraid that I would be left with no footing to get back to safety and the last comfortable place that I knew, that instead I would be relegated to the nowhere of failure, forever. The weight of the odds and obstacles was intense. At times, I'd want to quit even if just for some immediate relief.

This type of discouraging self-talk that I shared from my journal is one of the first elements to appear following a catastrophic failure or setback. It is our internal assessment of the situation and our triage center that determines the magnitude of the damage from the unwanted outcome. Some people are better than others at pushing it away quickly. I am not so lucky—I experience it all. So I use a process to make sure that I stay on forward track with my goals.

The Wall of Nevers

Disappointment stings. Perhaps as a protective mechanism, triggered by the pain, our self-talk intensifies to prevent us from ever finding ourselves in this type of discomfort again. So, immediately following a setback, the "Wall of Nevers" begins to arise.

"I'll never be able to do this."

"This will never work."

"I should have never tried."

"This will never get better."

Rather than providing an accurate assessment of the circumstances with the intention of moving forward, self-talk begins to amplify doubt with the actual purpose of preventing you from moving forward and trying again. Ironically, our self-protection mechanism is our own discourager-in-chief.

In spite of the setback, because we do still want the result of our dreams, we wind up profoundly hurt by the thinking that tells us not only will we never accomplish our goals we imagine, but it would be foolhardy to even try.

The real teeth of failure are that you've been judged to be insufficient in some way. You have no control over that judgment– it's just a grade. And you got an F. And you do have to process that F. You do have to sit with the loss and feel the sting and the burn of disappointment—letting yourself down, letting others down, not being able to hit the homerun the first time at bat. And it hurts. It's heavy and suffocating. But the feeling is *temporary*.

Reasons, Not Excuses

It is important to know that there is a difference between a reason for failure and an excuse, especially if you are competitive. An excuse—adopting the stance that in some way, your results or performance were entirely out of your control, robs you of the power to do things differently the next time. It is an escape from personal responsibility. On the other hand, a reason is a basis for learning in the future. It is an addressable condition that can be changed through directed effort. Afford yourself reasons, not excuses.

It Feels Worse When You See Others Succeed Where You Failed

As humans, we process and are influenced by what others do. If we see someone else doing it, it plants the seed to believe we can also do it. If we see someone else doing something we haven't done but want to do—or if it is something that we've failed at in the past, how do we change that process of interpreting what we saw and what it says about us and our potential?

I had to learn how to challenge the impulse to feel bad and to avoid translating the success of others who have progressed ahead of me into negative messaging about my own prospects. To do this, I conscientiously use the successes of other people as inspiration and a lesson for the future. Their success becomes a *template* to inform what I try next. If I see someone else do what I haven't or couldn't, I force myself to study what they *did* differently—not how they are different from me. This is helpful information for my next shot. If I'm not *given* a second chance, then it's my duty to make my second chance opportunity happen.

Seeing Other People's Success

The perfect opportunity to apply this lesson presented itself in the days following QVC. I had a smarting reminder that sometimes grand slams *are* hit the first time at bat when a friend debuted her product a few days following my appearance. While

53

my results were disappointing, her results were akin to hitting the game-winning shot of the championship in double overtime. No matter how much perspective you have, in the moment, when something you wanted to accomplish hasn't happened, seeing someone else do it or have it, feels like an insult to a painful injury. Reflecting about this in my journal. I wrote:

> This is a frustrating reminder that I have not reached my goal. So, practicing what I have been learning over these past few days in processing someone else's victory on the heels of my own defeat, I am rephrasing. I have not reached my goal yet. That's an important distinction. I will reach my goal—just along my own process and in my own way. It is something that I'm working for, but to have it in a way that doesn't compromise any of what is best for me. That means that it is going to take patience and a little more work.

Even more damaging, literally the next day, I had a phone call with another friend talking about two other similarly-situated beauty companies that had managed incredible and unbelievable sales numbers within their first 12 months of operation. Numbers that, in spite of doing well, we had not yet reached. Needless to say, the conversation, coupled with the circumstances was a lot. It left me feeling gutted, and I turned to my journal. Here's what I wrote:

> I was devastated. I felt like, well, why didn't I do that? How come I am not on that track? I felt like hearing their

story was an indictment of my performance, rather than bread-crumbs of information that could lead to me achieving my goal.

After all of this, the sale, QVC, the less than stellar results, coupled with other peoples' successes, it was overload and I had to take a step away for some breathing room. Later, in chapter 6, we'll explore what that looks like without losing momentum. Looking at the language I used in my journal, it's fairly easy to identify how I had internalized the information about other peoples' accomplishments and their success to negatively interpret my capabilities, preparedness, and competence. As an initial reaction, I saw their successes as a report that clearly indicated I had failed where others had succeeded. It took a lot of very intentional work to combat the negative self-talk that was triggered by these events. Not that I wasn't happy for others, but I was also still in a field of uncertainty about my own efforts. I couldn't yet see the *template* that was forming.

Even if the circumstances, information, and the people are different, we have a tendency to believe what we see and relate it to ourselves. Once we see it, we accept it as possible. Normally, that's an inspirational experience, especially if what we see is something that we never thought was possible, like going to the moon. It's inspirational if you're just watching on television. But, if you've spent years of your life training to be an astronaut, then every shuttle that leaves without you might feel like a missed opportunity. Now we see that it is possible, when we have not yet found the way, we wonder, *why wasn't it possible for me?* How you answer that question will help you understand how your self-talk works. If the answer to *why wasn't it possible for me?* Emphasizes something negative about you (e.g., I wasn't good enough, I am a failure, I'll never be able to get it done), then you probably have to shift your perspective.

Through regrouping, regardless of my natural inclination, I know that everything that we see, we should process as an inspiration. If we have envisioned something but haven't attained it yet, a similar success by another person should inspire us to know that success is possible. And, it shows at least *one way* that it can be done. Under the specific circumstances that we're observing (which are different from our own), it is possible, and now, we have the opportunity to figure out how to make it possible for our particular set of circumstances. We have the opportunity to customize the template created by their success.

In this age of social media, we are bombarded with constant images of other peoples' bright and shiny moments. We don't see them in the moments of work and struggle that it took to get there. We don't see the hours of preparation of hair and makeup to create one perfectly-lit image. And we certainly don't see the shots that didn't come out well. Given our understanding that we as humans do and want to do what we *see*, social media can be a gift and a curse. If you know how to use it as inspiration, it can motivate you to aim for new heights. If you do not, it can be one of the most powerful and unrelenting triggers to feeling inadequate—especially if what you see aligns with goals that you haven't reached *yet*. It's important to develop a method of survival in this space that we have collectively created for ourselves—a space in which we see the end product, the success presented to us as a flat 2-D image. We have to fill in for ourselves the background story of the work, sacrifice, and most importantly, the trial and error of failures that it took to get there.

Combating Defeating Self-Talk

I was visited by the most destructive and powerful self-imposed statement: "What's the point anyway?" The horrific "why try" statement that would serve to talk you out of all possibilities for success simply by discouraging a try. Why would you try if you think you may fail? Why try? Because what else will I do with my life? I'd rather ruin myself trying for the life of my dreams and a connection to my purpose than to wait out my time imprisoned by not taking my shot. I have to remember that. I had to remind myself. Why try? Because I can, that's why. If I fail, then I fail, but I will not decide to fail by deciding not to try. That, I will not do.

-- From my journal.

All Depends on Perspective

One year, I auditioned for *American Idol*. On the surface, it doesn't sound strange at all, *American Idol* was the top rated US television show for many of the 15 seasons that it ran. But, at the time, for the audition, I had to take a week off of my job as a music attorney to go, and it felt like a crazy thing to do.

It is much less the case now, but years ago, in the music industry, it was virtually unheard of and severely frowned upon to blur the lines between "talent and creative" and the "back-office and business" workers like I was. While it was acceptable for entry-level positions, at more senior levels, if your peers suspected that you wanted to transition from the business side to the talent side, they would certainly not take you seriously and would likely start to doubt your business acumen. It isn't accurate or fair, but it was the culture at the time. Now, years later, it is common to see the band performance fliers of many of my former executive-level colleagues from the music industry. It's wonderful to see how things change with time.

Over a decade ago, I was in my first real position in Los Angeles, just after passing the Bar Exam. It was a position that would re-launch my career as an entertainment attorney and executive after almost eight full months of random odd jobs and a grueling employment search that often left me exhausted and discouraged. I had worked as a tutor, as a marketer for a budding social network, and as a day performer for various television shows. Finally, working as a bona fide music attorney, after so many challenges, I desperately wanted to keep my job and earn the respect of my peers.

In spite of my new position and everything in my life seeming to line up in a particular direction after months of disarray, inside me, an unfulfilled dream nagged. When I was younger, I dreamed of being a singer. I used to sing along to Aretha Franklin's upbeat hits like "Freeway of Love" and Anita Baker's soulful ballads like "Caught Up in the Rapture." I would take the gigantic tape recorder that my mother had used to record her college lectures and record myself signing so that I could try to identify mistakes and improve. But, when I sang for family, no matter how much I had practiced, they all told me that I just didn't have the natural talent that it took to be a professional singer. So, I joined the choir at my church. In this way, I'd be able to sing amongst many other voices. Those that had so-called "natural talent" would drown out and carry over those of us who didn't. And despite numerous opportunities to sing a solo, I didn't, because I believed what I had accepted as wisdom greater than my own—that I was lacking natural talent and that natural talent was necessary to be a singer.

Although I trained myself to abandon my hopes, over the years, that itch continued to surface. While in law school, rather than taking notes, I started writing songs. Soon I had so many that I began working with a local producer to record them. I was told that my voice wasn't strong enough to carry the songs that I wrote, but still, I insisted on singing them on the recording anyway. But other than playing them for friends and family, the songs went nowhere.

So, years later, entrenched in a career and saddled with the debt of an expensive education, it felt extremely unrealistic to consider leaving the security of my very well-paying job to live the life of an aspiring singer. I needed a big shot, a "this is it" opportunity. And, *American Idol*, with its promise of immediate fame and income, seemed to be exactly the kind of opportunity I was asking for. It was a small sacrifice for a big chance. If I was *meant* to sing, I would wow the judges and have my shot on a huge national platform all while never missing a student loan payment. If I didn't make it, then at least I could tell myself I had tried to break out of the path of the *backoffice and business* side of the music industry and could face my fate with acceptance.

To help me prepare, my Dad called in a few favors and convinced some members of Aretha Franklin's team to listen to me practice my audition song. In retrospect, I should have been embarrassed—but, I wasn't. They said, politely, that I needed quite a bit more work on my… "technique." Undaunted, I, along with my mother and friend, drove from Michigan to Minneapolis for the audition.

Prepared, polished and wearing what I thought was a truly fabulous dress, I waited all day to finally stand in line on the floor of the arena to perform for the producers and production assistants. I didn't even make it past the first round. And I certainly never saw the infamous judge Simon Cowell. And just like that, after a day of waiting, and a lifetime of deferred dreaming, it was all over.

Even though my supposed "all or nothing" moment had failed, attempting to accomplish it still gave me the closure I needed. I could turn away from my singing ambitions and instead focus on excelling at the business and back-office aspect of the industry, with confidence that I was doing the right thing.

About a year later, my singing "bug" came back. Having been in LA for some time, I had the opportunity to speak with a successful professional singer who also teaches singing lessons. I explained that I would love to sing, but alas, I was not one of the lucky few born with the natural gift of song. I didn't have the talent. She *laughed.*

Finally, she said, "Girl, signing comes from the muscles in your throat and abdomen. And just like any of the other muscles in your body, they can be trained."

And then I realized, part of what I had been told, and what I had been telling myself about my abilities, this whole time, was untrue. Perhaps if I stayed stuck in the mindset and skillset that I held at that time, my story would have ended with a minor "ah-ha" and a still unfulfilled dream. But, with this *new* information, I realized that I had another shot at not having to live with that nagging bug of unmet desire. I took action and gave myself the gift of signing lessons. In the process, I found another local producer in LA to record a new set of songs. These were much better than my first set and this time, nobody even considered for a second that anyone should record them other than me. I don't have any interest in being a professional singer, but I can feel satisfied in learning what it would take to get there and removing the mental obstacles that would otherwise block my path. In return, I opened the door to an exciting new hobby, *fearless* karaoke, and an even better understanding of the production and creative side of the music business.

Negative self-talk serves a purpose. It protects us from pain and danger. It protects us from threats—both real and imagined. However, the concern with such talk arises when we allow the negativity to "protect" us by discouraging us from moving past a setback. Setbacks are real, but it is our mental and emotional reactions to failure that cause us to doubt ourselves and give up. The biggest threat to your success is letting the over-protective negative self-talk become amplified in the echo chamber of your own mind, making you give up on your dreams too quickly or too early.

Gift Yourself A Tool for Getting Better

Prior to my *American Idol* adventure, it never occurred to me to afford myself of the myriad of continuing education resources available, even to develop a persisting dream or hobby. Sure, I've had to take courses to maintain my license to practice law, and even had the fun of yoga and salsa dancing lessons, but prior to my singing lessons, if it wasn't for work or simple happenstance, it wasn't on my radar to pay to learn a new skill. Thankfully, my experience showed me that almost anything can be approached as a learned skill to develop. If you've run into the rut of a persistent setback, it is worthwhile to consider what might be a resource that can teach you an incremental skill or provide a piece of information to help you move forward or find a new path to try again.

Deliberate Constructive Self-Talk

We've all probably heard some version of "the power of positive thinking" as a prescription for success. This is also the antidote for defeating self-talk. Even in the early stages of mourning a setback, it is never too early to start nipping away at negative thoughts. Realistically, if you're anything like me, there is no way to stop defeating self-talk from happening. As we discussed above, it is an automatic action that stems from our natural self-protective mechanisms. So let's accept that there's no way around it. But, what you can do, knowing it is going to happen, is take quick, deliberate and affirmative steps to lessen its impact.

Self-Care:

It is only partly true that "time heals all wounds." Many times, the simple passage of time brings about healing and perspective to reduce the sting of negativity. The immediate threat is reduced, so your protective mechanisms relax a bit. The key with self-care and allowing the passage of time is to truly do nothing. Do not act on your defeating self-talk or overreact to it. If it helps, write your thoughts and feelings down, but do not take action on the negativity. It may help to remember that it is just your self-protection mechanism activating.

Mood Lifters:

What brings you joy? During this time, focus on actively doing things that will bolster your natural mood enhancers. Eat healthy and tasty foods you love, listen to your favorite music and dance, watch funny and uplifting movies, get active and moving—bring exercise endorphins into the mix. Get a massage or pampering to your taste—and, importantly, spend time around the most uplifting people you know, that you can count on for good, positive energy.

Start Winning:

Nothing outweighs a loss like a win. It may sound over-obvious, but in facing a setback, spend a little time winning at something very simple, where you can achieve a small, quick success. During my challenging times with Cosmedicine, I focused on brain games on the Lumosity platform. They were quick to play, I'd get a score and it was easy to see improvement from one day to the next. It didn't completely erase the pain of my circumstance, but it was a brief flicker of "feel good" that did its own small work in that moment. Set small goals and note your accomplishments. Decide to read a chapter of an uplifting book each day, and do it. Or make a plan to walk a mile a day. It doesn't matter what the specific goal is, but just the simple process of creating accomplishments for yourself starts to progressively ease and defeat the negativity in your mind.

Be Intentional About What You Tell Yourself:

Defeating self-talk arrives involuntarily. We can't control it. But what we can do is intentionally counteract a negative thought in our minds with an opposing and equally powerful positive thought. For example, if your mind is telling you, "I'll never get a job" counteract the thought by saying, "I am in control. If I don't get a job, I will make a job." If you can't think of anything positive, ask a friend to help and give you 5 positive things about you or your situation. Even if you don't believe them, repeat them to yourself. It's fair. Your mind is telling you all kinds of negative things that are untrue, so, you counteract by telling your mind all kinds of positive things that may not be true to you yet. By force of positive habit, you start to take the sting out of negative thinking.

Refocus on Your Goal or Dream:

When you experience a catastrophic failure, especially following what you believed was an "all or nothing" moment, it is easy to lose sight of your dream. To do this would be a mistake and would likely lead to you giving up. From the Beyoncé story, you see how easy it is to reduce your dream from wanting to be a star to the simplicity of wanting to win *Star Search*. No one opportunity is the totality of your dream. Putting so much mental weight on it as if it were everything can distort your vision. So, following a setback, make sure to reset the scale. Dial back into your original dream, before this one opportunity came about. Why did you pursue this opportunity? What was it that you wanted? Getting back to that place is important in that it will allow you to see the other opportunities waiting for you on the other side of the setback.

<u>Be of Service</u>:

It may seem very counterintuitive to consider reaching out to others to lend a helping hand, after *you* experienced a setback. At that time, you might feel like you need your own helping hand. When confronting a painful challenge, our first instinct is to draw in to ourselves, to make ourselves smaller, more compact – as if perhaps the pain we feel will shrink in proportion. But, the opposite is actually true. We heal best, especially in times of difficulty, by extending ourselves outward and helping others. Not only does it help shift the focus off of your personal burden, but it also feeds one of our basic human needs, to be valuable to others and to be of service.

The election of 2016 showed me the benefit of serving others better than I could have imagined. For my own reasons, the results of the 2016 presidential election hit me particularly hard. I was very upset on that night, and in the days that followed. Coupled with the various professional obstacles and setbacks I was simultaneously navigating, I felt violated, weak, defeated and nearly despondent. I wanted to stay in bed. I felt wounded and out of sorts, and I believed that there was no way beyond performing my basic responsibilities at work and at home, that I could find the strength to be of any help or service to anyone else—I had my own wounds to mend.

Then, I was reminded of a community service obligation that I had that upcoming Saturday. I had promised to co-lead a workshop at a community health fair, to help students navigate social media. There was an additional aspect of avoiding sex trafficking alongside representatives from a local non-profit that performed significant work in that arena. I was very hesitant to go. If I had not already promised, I'm not certain that I would have attended. As a specialist in business and branding for adults and organizations, I felt outmatched for the task of instructing middle schoolers.

Mentally and emotionally exhausted by my own circumstances, and consumed in my own story of challenge, I didn't *feel* like making the effort to do as good of a job as I wanted. And I certainly didn't want to sign on for any *extra* work. But, I had given my word about participating, and everyone involved encouraged me that the same principles that I espoused for complex objectives could be easily translated to keep those precocious little girls out of trouble. So, reluctantly, I went forward, uncomfortable, but willing. In the process, I learned how important it was to work to prevent the dangerous epidemic that sex trafficking has become in many communities around this country. Little did I know, it is an entire multibillion dollar industry happening while hidden in plain sight.

At 10:00 am on that Saturday morning, a young lady and her friend caught my attention. They were sitting alone in the first row of seats for our workshop. No one else had come in and we still were not scheduled to start for another 15 minutes. Several of us approached the young ladies to make sure that they were in the right place and to inform them of our starting time. One of the girls said, with determination, "I'm here for the sex trafficking workshop." She said it with such conviction, that all of us took particular notice. While a very important topic, usually young students do not pursue learning about sex trafficking with specific interest.

Our attention piqued, we began chatting, asking what she was hoping to gain. And it was in that conversation that I was forever changed. One of the young ladies had already been a victim of sex trafficking, and the other had been exploited via social media. They were both there because even though they survived those horrors, they wanted to learn what they could do to make sure that no other young girls or boys would face the same circumstances. Both of these young ladies were in foster care, and I learned that predators target children in special circumstances, where they believe that no one will come looking for them and where the promises that they make of living arrangements, money, clothes, phones and even love, would be received by hungry hearts.

In that workshop, my pain and suffering vanished, traded for an intensified connection to the world around me and an awareness of the responsibility that I must meet. If that young lady, facing those unbelievable circumstances had the courage, strength and energy to be of service to others, I could as well. I had no excuse to spend any more time absorbed in setbacks when I had something to offer others in need. It was a realization of the debt that I owe to my community, our children and our country to do my share to make the improvements that I can. I realized that no election was going to change this moment with these two young ladies in front of me. That responsibility for their education, protection and enrichment was ours as a community surrounding them. While we were meeting the call on that Saturday, the need would continue as would the duty. I may have been helpless to change the course of government at that time, but I was empowered to make a needed difference on Saturday and every day that followed.

As we wrapped up our seminar and the young ladies prepared to depart, I wished so badly that I could have taken them home with me. That I could have wrapped them up in a blanket of protection so that no harm or exploitation could erase the resolve and intention that they had set for themselves that day—that their own power and beauty would be preserved. But I couldn't. All I had to give was my book about social media, that I had written in 2012. I knew it was the best I had to give at that time. That day, I decided that I would write this book—to give the rest of what I had to offer—the lessons learned and insight gained following even more years of growth and experiences. It's the best I have as of now and my own act of service in these times.

As long as you have the gift of this day, you have options and opportunities. It is just up to you to learn how to see them. Once you have dialed back into your original vision, write it down and read it every day. Let it serve as a beacon to you as you pull yourself out of the discouragement and negative thinking of defeatist self-talk.

Chapter 3:
Separate Fact from Fiction

God grant me serenity to accept the things I cannot change;
courage to change the things I can; and wisdom to know the
difference

— Serenity Prayer

Nick Woodman is the CEO of GoPro, the maker of waterproof and mountable cameras and accessories that became wildly popular in the realm of action sports. GoPro is now a publicly-traded company with a $1.12 billion market cap and Nick Woodman is a billionaire, considered a success story by any measure.[10]

How GoPro came to exist is of particular interest in the

context of a Regroup, because it is the third-time venture for Nick, who failed previously in his first two, including funBug, an internet marketing company that had attracted venture investment funding.[11] When that enterprise failed as part of the dotcom bust, he was forced to sell the company at a fraction of the amount of the original investment, losing his investors' money. The experience of this letdown led him to vow not to rely on a similar structure for his next endeavor.[12]

Taking time to heal from the failure of his first company, Woodman set off on a surfing expedition, finding himself in Bali with his then-girlfriend (and now wife), Jill. Jill identified some handcrafted belts at the local market that she showed to Nick and described her ideas for making them even more appealing. Seeing a commercial opportunity in the belts, using his leftover savings, Nick ordered hundreds of them, at $1.90 a piece, to sell back in the US. Once their wholesale order arrived, Nick and Jill traveled up and down the coast of California in Nick's 1974 VW bus selling the belts for an unbelievable markup—at times for up to $60.[13]

These proceeds, coupled with a $35,000 loan that Woodman secured from his mother, allowed him to start building the prototypes for GoPro. He didn't let the first or second failures stop him. In fact, he used the lessons and experience to inform and build the third shot he took. It made him a billionaire. And from here, we can say, the rest is history.

When confronted with a setback, which can be a failure of some sort, running out of money, losing an important client, receiving a bad grade on a final, or even as significant as experiencing a miscarriage, that moment splits into two parts. The first part is, what happened. The second part is, what "what happened" means in the short and long terms. What happened is pretty easy to identify—it's a fact. However, because of our ever-efficient mind's protective mechanism, usually, the "what it means" portion gets wildly exaggerated and magnified out of context.

First Time is Usually Not the Charm

Every day we are inundated with the virtual highlight reels of everyone around us. We see the edited and sterilized versions of others' lives. For some reason, we want to only share our high points with others, as the risk of the vulnerability of exposing the low points presents a real fear of shame, negative perception and "reputational" risk. And even worse, that we might do damage to our "brand." Further, the press focuses its attention not on struggles in progress, but struggles completed and generally the information we receive deprives us fully of the parts of our collective experience that we could truly learn from.

A study by Francine Lafontaine and Katherine Shaw was recently covered in *Bloomberg*. In it, they followed a set of Texas entrepreneurs for over 20 years. In their findings, during that period, 91.7% of the 2.4 million businesses that were started failed.

75% of those new businesses were started by first-time entrepreneurs with no prior experience. Here's what's interesting: once failure happened, 71% of those first-timers stopped right there. They didn't try another businesses after the first one failed. Too bad for them, because for the 29% that did try again, they showed an increased likelihood of success in their later ventures. In fact, their probability of having a successful venture increased the more times they tried.[14] Based on these results, success certainly doesn't look like getting it right on your first shot. Success looks like taking your knocks, and trying again.

Below, I'm going to talk through some of the work of separating what is real from what is imagined. The success bias all around us is certainly real, I even read it in my own journal. It gives us a false impression of the gravity of impact of our own shortcomings and fosters unwarranted feelings of inadequacy and helplessness. In a later chapter, I will walk through more specifically how to combat fueling the defeating self-talk that results from seeing the accomplishments of others. But for now, we're going to start with the simple process of distinguishing what is real, from what is not.

Reality Check

By now, I think that we can agree on a few things:

<u>First</u>, setbacks happen along the path to success. The bigger the opportunity, following a negative result, the larger the setback feels.

<u>Second</u>, most setbacks begin with a deluge of negative self-talk which, while serving a self-protective function, can also be debilitating and discouraging.

<u>Third</u>, what you do with the negative self-talk is going to determine if and how you move forward.

You can't simply think positive thoughts when a setback happens. That is only part of the equation for improving your mind state. The second half is, as your defeating self-talk is a protection mechanism, that it is protecting you from something. The fear that is being elicited has a real foundation; however the defeating self-talk serves to amplify it to unrealistic levels, beyond the actual magnitude and nature of the threat. It overstates the consequences and uses any available "fuel" (e.g., social media posts, news stories, comparisons to other people) as reinforcement. As we've explored in previous chapters, in reality, the deluge of damming consequences and definitive negative conclusions (e.g., I can't, I shouldn't, it won't) are largely unfounded and have the potential to obscure your options.

Buried within that barreling snowballing myth of imminent danger, failure and certain demise, all created by your mind, there is a small grain of truth about what you should *actually* worry about. Your job is to find that grain, and only that grain.

Just before starting GoPro, when Nick Woodman's second venture failed, he was concerned about having lost other peoples' money. He surely felt defeated when he set off on a surfing expedition for self-care and healing. But along the way, he discovered and dealt with the root of the fear driving his self-defeating talk—the fear that his failures would hurt others by costing them their money. He then found a way to generate enough start-up capital by himself such that he could manage his own risk. At least this way, if he failed, he would fail on his own terms and with his own investment.

Once we find a way to lighten the heavy burden of negative thinking, we then need to take the next step of actually assessing true consequences and legitimate fears from a realistic perspective. This requires a focus on objective facts, not perceptions or guesses based on incomplete information. For example, a loss of money is a fact—you have a tangible dollar amount that you can reference. However, loss of reputation, meaning that you believe that people think less of you, is what I call perception damage. You do not actually know what other people think of you, and until you find out, you have incomplete information. Many times, we spiral far beyond the facts of our individual situation, which really at the center is just a small, recoverable kernel of loss. This kernel, when magnified by our own thoughts and our assumptions about what people think or what may happen subsequently, takes on a life of its own, snowballing into a vicious monster, tearing at your confidence and resolve until you're defeated into submission and completely discouraged from moving forward.

The objective of changing this type of thinking, and focusing on the actual damage (i.e., damage you can specifically identify and/or quantify), can serve to lighten the load and prevent the monster from even appearing. This is the best way to keep things in perspective.

Following a setback, ask yourself:

Is my freedom affected? Have I lost or will I lose my freedom?

For many, this may seem like a strange consideration. But freedom is one of the most fundamental aspects of our human needs and desires. This is not lifestyle freedom, or the ability to do whatever you want, whenever you want, wherever you want. This is the most basic concept that you have not been stripped of your freedom through some official process.

With freedom, even in the most challenging of circumstances, we are still at liberty to make decisions for ourselves. To varying extents, we can control our geography and what we do with our time. Having the power of choice is the seed upon which many promising futures are built, even if the seed is tiny at first. So, if you have freedom, you still have a wide range of options and choices—a place to start or restart and something to be grateful for.

Even those whose freedom is extremely limited have found a way to create options for themselves. I think of the story of Wahida Clark, who, while serving a 10-year sentence for a non-violent crime, became a bestselling author, launching a popular book series behind the walls of a prison. As well, there is the story of Piper Kerman, who used her experience in a Federal Penitentiary to form the basis of what we know as the extremely popular Netflix series *Orange is the New Black*.

I am not advocating pursing a vision or dream that will put you at the risk of losing your freedom. In fact, to the contrary. This just represents the most extreme and severe type of setback—baseline zero, so to speak. And if options can be created from this place, you should have certainty that options can be created from where you stand following your own setback of a lesser degree.

Is my health affected? Did I damage my body or health?

In addition to freedom, in order to exercise the fullest reach of our opportunities for choice and self-determination, we need to focus on maximizing our health. We might have varying abilities and limitations, varying degrees of wellness and energy, but with breath in our bodies and air in our lungs, we have the fullest potential of each moment before us. We hear of extraordinary feats of will by people like Stephen Hawking, the theoretical physicist whose body might be constrained but whose mind certainly has no limits. If the setback you faced has left your health and body intact, you have cause to celebrate.

Is my family affected? Did I injure emotionally or physically anyone that I care about?

In certain circumstances of setback, we negatively affect people we care about. This is different from considering how they *think* of us, meaning we've lost their respect or esteem. This is a circumstance, similar to Nick Woodman's, in which we've lost our family's money or otherwise damaged an important relationship because of a failed enterprise. With most setbacks, the injury faced is borne by us alone, and the damage is internal. So, if you have not hurt anyone you care about along the way, consider how many inadvertently have, and yet still managed to repair the relationships, return the investments (many times over), and resolve conflicts just by continuing the pursuit of their goals. Relationships can be repaired and money can be recovered. But having the right perspective will be the key to sustaining the course needed to progress forward to better times and circumstances.

Is my financial security affected? Have I lost money or will I need money?

Consequences that affect your financial security are a common concern following a setback. Nick Woodman needed to raise money independently. For others, the consequences could be more severe. Beyoncé's family at one point lost their home. In a moment after my first job ended, I found myself down to my last dollar. Money can always be made, and, for those that have learned, *saved* to lighten the impact of setbacks along your path. We'll discuss maintaining savings as a mechanism for creating options in a separate chapter, and how this can be a powerful tool in your arsenal when it comes time to regroup.

Reconnecting to Reality

Focusing on the reality of your circumstances is the first step to actually surmounting them. You need your true coordinates. While your mind might be telling you all kinds of horrific stories about what will or could happen (e.g., "No one will ever invest in you again," "People will think you're an idiot," "Your partner is going to leave you") none of these things are true if they have not happened. They may be *possible*, but they are not *true*. Your job is to weed out the exaggerations and conjecture about what could possibly happen so that you have the strength and energy to deal with what *actually has* happened. The best and most logical predictor of what may happen is to look at what actually has happened. It's never as bad as the negative self-talk is telling you that it is.

It makes me uncomfortable, scared even, not being able to feel the certainty of the ground beneath my feet. Following any setback, I often find myself having to resist the urge to limit my upward climb in favor of looking for what I can identify as more stable ground. But, then I ask myself, *why do I have the urge to quit before I've actually hit a wall?* Is it because I'm uncomfortable with the discomfort? I've wondered if it is because the most accessible and easiest path to safety I know is to think back to when I wasn't feeling this way – before I had reached for something more. Incidentally, this is also when I was bored, safe, and cocooned in what felt like a prison of comfort. *Do I really want to go back to a time when all I wanted was a chance to take my shot?* Ironically, these were the times when I knew the fullest comfort, and yet, as an adventurer, it was comfort that made me feel like I was dying on the inside.

One of my father's favorite sayings is that sometimes you have to get comfortable with being uncomfortable. To make any progress toward our dreams, life often forces us to learn a new thing, to find a new system and routine, which brings about change and challenge. This is our opportunity to develop a new way of processing the feelings of discomfort – so that we can tell ourselves a new story about what the uncertainty means and what is to come. This is our opportunity to Regroup, to find a new comfort in the uncomfortable and uncertain.

Never giving up does not mean that you never encounter failure, and it doesn't mean that you don't *want* to quit. It is about refusing to quit *just because* you're uncomfortable. In a time of failure or uncertainty, it is about refusing to be dominated by the inertia of negative thinking and willing your mind to find the resolve and commitment to try again.

Contingency Plan

"Each day brings its own perils and its own courage afresh."

Once you have identified the *true* and *immediate* consequence(s) of the setback, the next step is to start working on a contingency plan to deal with those consequences. The most common consequence of our individual setbacks is money-related. A good friend of mine told me once that any money you have is a temporary solution to a permanent problem. You'll always need it—the only difference is when and how much. Earl Nightingale, a mid-century prosperity thinker who wrote and recorded *The Strangest Secret* advised his audience to save 10% of their incomes as a backup. Having a pool of capital that you can use allows for instant access to options once you have a plan in place to address the consequences of a setback.

After I learned to save and create adequate reserves for myself, the sting of risks that didn't work out was substantially reduced. Instead, my savings served as my own personal investment fund. I used them whether I wanted to buy something as small as a new domain name, or a course for new skills, to fund web or application development, or simply to buy myself some time to think. This is going to be the most important tool in your arsenal to navigate the uncertainties along your path. You can't predict the future, or prepare your way out of *all* risk, but you can learn and develop the skill of saving as a method to increase your options and create opportunities when you need to.

Our inflow of income forms the basis of stability. When a scenario is presented that threatens that flow, our first thought, rather than options or opportunity, is how to survive. How you handle this moment is crucial to whether or not you'll be able to Regroup successfully. Survival mode is a crippling state that denies us access to our creativity and optimism. It is a painful, bare-bones mode accompanied by a selfish, small, and self-defeating attitude. It's like being in a car stuck in first gear when you really need to accelerate to win a race from behind. The key is to get out of this mode as quickly as possible.

I know this feeling of survival mode quite well, and I've had to learn how to climb my way out of it. During one of my first layoffs, I was making so little money, that I hadn't really had an opportunity to amass significant savings. I panicked and my mind took me on a horrific and frightening journey through the future that was to come for me, of continued joblessness, losing my apartment, having to move back in with my parents and being limited in all other aspects of my life. In the time since, I've learned how to establish and maintain savings, and later to create jobs and revenue for myself and for others, and I now have many more resources to stop me from retreating to survival mode upon a setback. But, it didn't start out that way and it hasn't fully eliminated occasions of paralyzing concern. While the panic and mental impulse to retreat and just survive never fully goes away, we can learn to change our response to gradually reduce the amount of time between panic and planning.

In the circumstances that I've previously described, when thoughts swirled in my head of losing my company and my job, to ease the anxiety and find actionable steps, I forced myself to drill down into what that kind of setback would actually mean. First, losing a job would mean losing income. Yet, with my resources, knowledge and experience, generating income would not be a challenge. I happen to specialize in business architecture, professionally. So, most important for me was to figure out how much *time* I would need to develop and execute my next plan along the way to my goals. From previous experience, that amount of time was three months, but I used a figure of six months for safety. Some people, based on their current skills and experience might need more time, or less. Making this determination for yourself, alleviates uncertainty by creating a realistic *factor of safety*. Just don't push yourself into paralysis by needing to be *too* safe. You'll never be able to save enough to eliminate *all* risk.

Armed with an estimate of how much time I would need, the next step was to create a monthly budget so I could work my way into a final figure for my "safety net." Having had the benefit of a generous salary, I had not been previously keeping detailed account of my spending. To eliminate any uncertainty, I tallied all of my expenses, absolutely *everything* I could think of that I would need for a given month, including costs for time with friends and family. Once I had that number, I multiplied it by the six months I estimated were needed to regain my footing. Having the certainty of that final budget amount made me relieved and gave me a powerful weapon against the fear rattling in my mind.

With my safety net number, and a little bit of headspace for breathing room, I immediately set about making sure that that budget was either allocated and present in my savings, or could be reached in the amount of time that I could still count on with my income. I had to immediately stop frivolous and non-essential spending. I made a list of all of my liabilities and assessed what I could eliminate and how much I could save. Even before it was made certain that I would need to, taking Earl Nightingale's advice to heart, I shoveled money into savings and calculated what other amounts I might need as a launchpad for my next endeavor. It was a bit of a sacrifice, but well worth it in the end. Getting a head start on unfavorable circumstances makes a big difference. I started on my plan based on just the inkling that I would need it.

If you pick just one change of your own to make today, it should be to take action sooner. Don't wait. How many times do we see the writing on the wall but wait for the sledgehammer to fall before we move? Move now.

Once I made my plan, every day that followed counted as a drop in my bucket of newfound certainty and security in the midst of uncertainty and chaos. I still wasn't sure how things would turn out based on circumstances, but I had already positioned myself to rise out of survival mode and to begin to consider opportunities and plans for the future. The destructive thoughts of doom and the anxiety released into a fledgling sense of excitement. I had created a plan to *buy* myself enough time to handle my own Regrouping *if* the event that I feared the most came to pass. And each further day that it did not, was another step towards victory over circumstances that I could not control.

By getting to the root of my concern and addressing my worst fear, I became free of it and was ready to tackle the next hurdle with my mental and emotional energy intact. The six months that I bought for myself was enough time to get me out of the panic of immediate survival mode and to start thinking about options and the possibilities that could lead me closer to what I actually wanted.

While many setbacks result in terrible financial consequences, the missing resource for some of the more challenging setbacks is knowledge. This shows up as unexpected obstacles that we have *no idea* how to tackle. In fact, given our current knowledge resources at the time, it would be fair to say that these kind of obstacles and the odds of surmounting them are impossible.

If It Wasn't Impossible...

At Cosmedicine, one of our greatest goals was our relationship with QVC, and certainly, one of our greatest successes was our debut product launch on that channel. While many saw my appearance that night, what they did not see was the 11 months of work that it took to get there, and the stack of "impossible"-made-possible obstacles that we crossed in the process.

One of my favorite memories of that time is about a surprise obstacle we conquered, a required packaging modification to meet QVC's guidelines. When we received word that we would have to make some adjustments to fit with QVC's robust quality assurance process, as a small company, we felt like we had reached an end. We would have to individually address hundreds of product units at an undetermined cost if we were to move forward. I recall vividly the moment in which we were informed that there was no other way to progress.

On the telephone with my colleague, as I sighed with the resignation of defeat, she had another perspective entirely. While a bit winded from the overwhelming nature of the task at hand, she seemed to be almost cheerful as we discussed our next steps. Meanwhile, I couldn't get past the fact that we were lacking in both resources and knowledge as far as how to proceed. Even though I could not see a way forward, the fact that another person was looking hopefully at the same circumstances that I considered impossible prevented me from closing the door of my mind to *curiosity*.

Emotionally exhausted and spent, I stepped away and took a break. I closed my eyes for a nap, hoping to push from my mind all thoughts of this impending defeat on the heels of our coming so close to tasting success. And if I'm being totally honest, I'll tell you, I never even made it to my bed. I had been so winded by the bad news that I actually made a surprisingly graceful crumbling collapse to the floor of my apartment and stayed there until I fell asleep. It was *that* bad.

A few hours later, still intending a mental escape from the circumstances, my mind kept drifting back to a single question: *well, if it weren't impossible, how would you go about it?* And I'd *laugh* to myself—*it is impossible, so no sense in thinking about it.* But the question kept coming back – dancing around inside my mind. I didn't realize it at the time, but this simple and persistent question was the earliest seed of a plan beginning to form. Even in the darkest hour, *curiosity*, can make its own way.

This early plan, which at the beginning, was just an unquench-able question, started to grow in my mind. And soon, *"If it isn't impossible, then how would you go about it?"* began to morph into *"It isn't impossible. How would you go about it?"* And boy did that question have answers. A few at first were ridiculous. But each one of those answers was a little light in the darkness, leading the way to a better and more definitive answer. Soon, I was inspired enough to do some research and develop my knowledge and re-sources. Before I knew it, I had a plan, a fully-developed, execut-able and realistic plan that started from impossible circumstances. Nobody could tell us how to do it, but eventually we figured it out. And it was all with the help of a tiny persistent question and a curiosity that refused to die down.

We hit even more hiccups along the way to our airdate, but none were insurmountable. Once we had tackled that first "impossible"—the one that threatened to derail our efforts—the others were easier to challenge and address. Never giving up sometimes looks like almost giving up but the key is holding on to hope and curiosity.

Opportunity Calling

I can genuinely say that I have never met a person who was not at all resilient. Simply living life on a daily basis requires nothing less. But when it comes to living a life that is meaningful to you and that reflects the dreams that only you know about, the obstacles are larger and come with more of an emotional burden. These are the challenges significant enough to knock the wind out of your sails and send you spiraling without direction. These are the moments that make you feel a sense of lost footing as you're climbed far above the safety of familiar grounding. But the spaces beyond familiar ground are where character is developed and the greatest truth of who we are and who we were meant to be is found.

Without practice, it can feel overwhelming. For me it did. When I took my first leap, in the days before I had savings or a regular income, or had even spent a full year at a regular job, I had no idea what I was capable of and didn't trust my own ability or will.

In the present for you, and for many others, the tools you need, like savings, for example, might be simply a wish. The safety net that you have may not even get you past today. But even this is *not* a stopping point — it is just the start. Perhaps you have to take a job — a job that you don't like or don't want, similar to what I did following the folding of my first position at the music startup. Perhaps you have to develop a new skill. The temporary sacrifice of the actual day-to-day experience may be unpleasant, but once you have a purpose that you're working toward, it becomes bearable – you have your *why*.

Imagine creating a job for yourself based on a need that you're able to identify. As an example, consider the ingenuity of my neighbor. I came to know her because we lived on the same floor and for some reason, our schedules seemed to be synchronized. When I was in the elevator, so was she. When I walked in from the garage, she was also there. We saw each other so many times that we began to chat. After about the third encounter, she offered me her card for private pilates training. I thanked her, but let her know that pilates just wasn't a form of exercise I could wholeheartedly subscribe to—and certainly not at the cost of private lessons. It was an easy and friendly conversation between neighbors who would most certainly see each other again.

One day, a couple of months later, we ran into each other again, this time, at the mailboxes. I was checking my mail after walking my dog. My neighbor, said hello and then added, "Oh by the way, here's my new card. I'm a dog walker now." I looked up, my interest piqued. She continued, "since so many people here have dogs, I thought I would lend my services." Well, she had hit squarely at the center of something that mattered to me. With my dog leash in hand, we proceeded to have a conversation about rates. This story just goes to show that opportunities are right in front of your nose, if you're paying attention to the needs of those around you.

What if This is It?

I have more perspective on it now, but I will never forget the soul-sucking monotony of the seemingly endless work I had to face following the folding of my first startup position. I would spend up to 18 hours a day, sitting in front of a computer screen, with limited access to the internet, clicking through document after document and checking boxes for litigation discovery. In my spirit, I wanted to build an entertainment empire, but my body and at least a part of my mind were relegated to the constraints of a chair in the monotone grey interior of an office building, all while the constant flickering of the overhead florescent lights seemed to taunt me.

When I think about it now, I can still connect to the despair I felt when my mind would occasionally wander to the place of questioning, *what if this is it?* The mere thought of spending the remainder of my days doing this work just to survive was heavy and depressing. What pulled me out of my funk every time, was my focus on my why, my purpose and my plan. I'd go through my list every day in my mind, and when times really got rough, when I really felt my hope slipping away, I'd do it again. I'd tell myself:

I'm getting up today and going to this place because I am working to save money. I am saving money because I am moving to California. I am moving to California because I am going to fulfill my dream of building an entertainment empire and there I will have the resources and opportunities to make it come true. And so, I am getting up today and going to this place because I am building an entertainment empire.

When I got really bored, I added in another low-level goal that I could work on simultaneously while I was stuck in my contingency plan. I had been planning to shed a few extra pounds, so I started myself on a diet and made a goal of drinking 100 oz. of water a day while I was sitting at my job. It was easy because I had access to a kitchen (and a restroom, necessarily). I made it work.

Everyone's situation is different, and just as mine was terrible to me, I realize that other people face much more significant hurdles and circumstances more challenging than my own. I can only imagine what someone else's contingency plan might require them to do. I think of the story of Khadijah Williams, who spent much of her early life homeless — but clung to the promise of hope that education brought. In spite of attending 12 schools over a span of 12 years, through determination and sheer force of will, she was able to create enough stability for herself to earn admission to Harvard in her senior year of high school. In spite of the setbacks presented each time that her family was forced to move out of their shelter, or car or other temporary living accommodations, Khadijah had to find a way to ensure that she could maintain her placement in the public schools' gifted and talented program and her near-perfect G.P.A. Of the public library, she said: "The library gave me some control over some aspect of my life. Even though I couldn't really control where I would live or anything, I could control how much I wanted to learn."[15] And even with its most incredible nature, Khadijah's story is far from being the only one with similar details.

The realistic answer to "what if I fail" is that the reality of certain setbacks and hurdles must be acknowledged and confronted. There are very real consequences and possible damages to what you may attempt if your efforts fall short. But for every problem there is a solution. The key is to separate fact from fiction and to distinguish what is real from what is really only in your mind.

Strengthening Your Resolve

Contingency planning and problem solving take me back to our friend Thomas Edison. All the accounts that I had previously read about his life as an inventor and his incredible body of work, seemed to have left out the fabulously unique personality he showed to those in his closest confidence. M.A. Rosanoff, Edison's lab chemist, wrote an account for *Harper's* Magazine in 1932, describing Edison's reaction to Rosanoff's own frustrations as a young scientist trying to impress his boss. New to his position, he had spent a considerable amount of time working on a lab assignment yielding no solution or results.[16] The stakes were pretty high given that Edison was a big-time famous inventor and Rosanoff, who had just finished school, had been hired by circumstance on a whim. As this very first assignment, Rosanoff was tasked with developing a perfected wax, that was neither too soft nor too hard, that could be used for the cylinders that were read by Edison's invention, the phonograph, to reproduce music. These were the first musical recordings in our society. The original wax worked ok, but when a loud noise was played on a recording, its hardness would cause a microscopic shattering, causing later distortions in the playback. A softer wax would avoid this and help maintain audio fidelity over repeated plays.

Rosanoff worked on this for months and months. In fact, for his entire recounting of his time with Edison, over pages and pages of entertaining encounters, he still hadn't figured out how to master that "damn" wax. Edison used to cajole him based on his theoretical education, and extolled the benefits of a practical and experiential one - as if having more practical experience would have caused Rosanoff to think more openly about problem-solving and what could and could not be done. In Edison's perspective, it must have been the formal education that ruined

Rosanoff's creative thinking. After some time, poor Rosanoff, discouraged by his lack of results was about ready to throw in the towel and put the label of "impossible" on his project. He went to Edison with this decision, labeling his efforts a "wild goose chase."

Edison for his part, listened intently (with much concentration, as he had lost a considerable portion of his hearing), and then said, "I've been in the inventor business for over thirty-tree [sic] years, and my experience is that for every problem the Lord has made me he has also made a solution. If you and I can't find the solution, then let's honestly admit that you and I are damn fools, why blame it on the Lord and say He created some[thing] impossible – a problem that's got no solution?"[17]

Following that conversation, our chemist, Mr. Rosanoff, perhaps not convinced by Edison of anything other than Edison's conviction itself, returned to the lab to continue to work on his *impossible* wax problem. One day—and there was literally nothing particularly special about this particular Sunday—Rosanoff, in a haze of cigarette smoke, reposed on his sofa, nursing a headache had a flash of inspiration about the solution. He had worked so hard and so long on his problem. He had immersed himself in it and finally, gave himself over to it, being held to the fire by his quirky, yet insightful boss. In doing so, he had figured it out. Given time and continued effort, a refusal to believe in the impossible caused his breakdown to result in a breakthrough.

This story is a reminder that what we deem impossible is as much a choice as deciding to carry on in our pursuits. Failure and giving up is as much a faith as is faith in the positive outcome. Both hinge on a belief about what has not yet happened. Both fill in the blank of an unknown future result. Edison's faith about a positive outcome, for the solution to the problem, governed his interpretation of the facts. Meanwhile, Rosanoff's "faith" about a negative outcome, governed his interpretation of not only the problem before him, but the results he had achieved to that point. It was only after Edison pushed him "back in the ring," that Rosanoff was able to afford himself the additional effort needed to reach the solution. He put more work in, and finally, at the right moment, the right thought arrived. It was inevitable as Edison believed it, and history has shown this to be true.

> *"Many of life's failures are people who did not realize how close they were to success when they gave up."*
> – Thomas Edison

There is a story in Napoleon Hill's classic book *Think and Grow Rich* that speaks of the idea of being just "three feet from gold."[18] In the story, a man, R. U. Harby, staked his fortunes on prospecting for gold, during the gold rush of the 1920's. After digging, his uncle seemed to have found an untapped vein of ore running underground. Imagine their elated excitement in unlocking the door to unimaginable wealth – what a prize! All that they would need to do now, is dig. After raising money for the needed machinery, Hardy and his uncle devoted their full effort to mining the precious metal. At first, things were going quite well, as expected. They were able to make enough money to pay off a considerable portion of debt and seemed well-positioned to imminently strike it rich. Except, all of a sudden, one day, without warning, they reached the end of the ore they had found. The supply ended entirely unexpectedly. In spite of continuing efforts to dig and find where it picked up again, they found nothing. Convinced that their findings were conclusive and permanent, they accepted failure and in defeat, sold their digging machinery for almost nothing.

But while they gave up, the purchaser of their efforts was just getting started. Convinced that there was more gold to be found, he hired a mining engineer to do a survey of the land. The engineer investigated the mine and showed, according to his calculations, just three feet away from where Harby and his uncle stopped digging, the vein of gold began again. Because of the proximity to a fault line, the earth in that area wasn't even, and the gold began just three feet lower than expected. As you can imagine, this discovery generated millions, just not for Harby, or his uncle.

How many times have we decided prematurely that something is impossible because we were lacking knowledge? How easy is it to put in the work, either to improve ourselves or to increase the amount of information that we possess? Then, to make the decision to keep on digging? Knowing where you want to go, coupled with the positive faith that you can get there, will help provide the fuel to move past setbacks, even when it seems that you've run out of options.

Armed with a refocused vision, a realistic understanding of the actual consequences of your setback and a contingency plan, you are much further along the path than most people ever get towards accomplishing their dreams. If you can manage not to give up at the beginning, you start to develop the habits that will ensure that you see your way through to the end.

REFRAME

Chapter 4:
Debrief

Sometimes, at the conclusion of a project, wise leaders schedule a debrief. A debrief brings all of the players back together to talk about what they did, how they did it and to extract the lessons for the future. In a world where we tend toward moving on quickly once something is done, a debrief requires to you linger just a little longer and put in some extra work—for yourself. During a debrief, everyone on the team is expected to undertake a methodical process of determining what happened during the experience and how they felt along the way. Then through an analytical process, asking questions, and examining thoughts, behaviors and decisions, they evaluate the experience to identify the lessons that can be learned for the future.

The process of a debrief can also be used personally to properly extract the valuable lessons presented during a challenge and to inform your plan for the future, even if you do it on your own with just your journal as your witness.

Dr. James Pennebaker, a social psychologist, researcher and professor at the University of Texas at Austin has conducted some very interesting experiments on the effects of expressive writing on both emotional and physical well-being, as well as on tangible positive professional results, such as being rehired after a layoff.

In an early study, while researching people with terminal illnesses and autoimmune disorders, he found that by simply giving patients an exercise to write out their thoughts and emotions in the context of receiving treatment, those who did so tended to fare better in managing the symptoms of their illness. Even HIV patients found their immune system counts higher than those who had not pursued the same outlets.[19]

Dr. Pennebaker's subsequent study, "Expressive Writing and Coping with Job Loss," details the astonishing result that proved that people who write about their thoughts and emotions relating to a job loss (i.e., *expressive writing*) are prone to be rehired faster than those who do not.[20]

In the experiment, 63 individuals affected by a layoff, ranging in age from 40 to 68 years, and who had been working for an average of 20 years for their former employer, were given the option to participate in a writing exercise as part of their outplacement support activities. Of the 63 people in the study, 20 were in the group that would engage in the *expressive writing* exercise. The control group, consisting of 21 people, would also write, but only about basic objective details, such as the activities that they had planned for each day generally, or as part of the search for employment. The remaining 22 individuals in the group, would be non-writers, serving as a control group to measure against the expressive writing group.

After the first three months of the experiment, in the expressive writing experimental group, 5 individuals had gotten new jobs; none in the writing control group and 2 in the non-writing control group. After eight months of the experiment, 10 out of 19 of the expressive writers (one dropped out) had found full-time employment, as compared to only 5 of the 21 writing control group subjects and 3 of the 22 non-writing control subjects. In fact, the results were so clear that the experiment, originally designed to continue for a year, was stopped after this time so that all of the participants, including those in the control groups could take part in the obvious benefits of expressive writing in their own job searches.

The other aspect of these results to note is that those in the expressive writing group were not observed to send any more letters, make any more contacts or receive any more phone calls from prospective employers than those in the other groups. It seems that the results were merely a function of the psychological benefit to be gained from writing out an account of events along with your corresponding thoughts and feelings.

Making a detailed account also serves to preserve the record of what happened so that you'll remember it later, as a study has shown that adults tend to forget an average of three things a day.[21] According to the company 3M, the maker of Post-it notes, who conducted their own study of 2,000 adults, we forget up to four.[22] You don't want that to include the valuable details which can later lead to benefits for you and others, as you learn from your experiences. Moreover, a different study done by scientists at the University of Basel in Switzerland showed that the human brain actually *needs* to forget unimportant details in order to remain efficient.[23] Wondering what is unconsciously deemed unimportant by your body's clearing mechanisms? You lose the details that you don't focus on. It's a true "use it or lose it" type of system. For that reason, in order to make sure that you'll be able to use it in the future, you'll need to make sure that the record is there.

This is also an interesting explanation for why the advice about success from so many well-known and notable achievers tends to seem so general. It may very well be that the passage of time from their formative struggles has erased details of the valuable portions of their experience. They now overlook those details in favor of recalling and recounting bigger challenges that are hard to relate to.

The Accounting at Work

Hoping for raw insight on the process of working through a setback, especially one that didn't end with a big boring bow tied around it, I started looking for stories. I found a writer on *Medium*, Hampus Jakobsson, who had courageously written about the folding of his second startup, a software product called Brisk.[24] His first company, The Astonishing Tribe, or TAT for short, after having developed nearly the entire user interface for the first iteration of Google's Android platform, was acquired by Blackberry. On the heels of this success, Jakobsson set about developing a brand new idea. Having had the benefit of a prior positive outcome and the supposed wisdom and resources that it afforded, it was unthinkable to him that this next adventure would lead to an entirely undesirable result.

While many startups fold, an estimated 90% of them, what made Jakobsson's story of Brisk unique was not only the candor with which its founder and CEO described the actual process of folding, but also the instructional visibility provided into how he and his team approached the process of failure. They decided to shut down the company in a way that would prove rewarding and beneficial for all involved, even though the decision had been made not to continue their original operations as planned. He and his team actually made a plan to *fail well*.

In an insightful Medium post entitled "How We Debriefed

When Our Startup Folded," Hampus details the steps that his team undertook to gainfully work through shutting down everything they had been working on over the prior three years.[25] The first step? Taking an accounting of what happened. Not just an accounting of the actual failure(s), but of *everything* that happened. The good, the bad, the ugly and everything in-between.

In fact, along with the suggestions I've detailed, it was this post by Jakobsson that inspired me to keep up a regular practice of writing in my own journal. So, I started a renewed focus on recording in real time, not just the events of my period of setback, but also my thoughts and emotions that were stirred as well.

Facts Matter

As you might be starting to realize, giving up versus not giving up is less about your circumstances and more about the battle that rages between the part of your mind that you control, vs. the part of your mind that you do not. To be fully equipped to separate facts from the fiction that your mind creates, you will need to mine for the actual facts of your circumstance. A well-known and well-regarded study by Phillip Ulrich and Dr. Susan Lutgendorf from the University of Iowa shows specifically that writing that includes facts alongside an articulation of thoughts and feelings have a more effective result in improving the wellbeing of the person keeping the journal.[26] This benefit of expressive writing is a result that parallels and reinforces the Pennebaker job search study discussed earlier.

In a moment of loss or setback, we tend to focus on the negative circumstances and emotions and forget the positive. And the reality is that for virtually every endeavor that you will undertake, there is good that comes along with the bad. Even if it is 95% bad and only 5% good, if you can find the good and focus on it, you can enlarge that good. To do that, you'll need an accounting of your facts.

Write it Down

Given the discomfort of a painful experience, we often look for the most expeditious way to alleviate that pain. Many times, this means that we want to just "move on" quickly and mentally "throw" the entire experience away, including the proverbial *baby* with the *bathwater.*

You might mistakenly believe that because the experience ended with a painful result, there is nothing to be gained from it and holding on to any piece of it will prevent you from doing the work that you need to heal. If you do this, you risk not receiving the benefit of mining all of the valuable insights to be gained from your experience. Don't just move on—*move through.*

Creating your accounting might be the easiest element of your Regroup. Whether you are in the middle of a challenge, deciding whether to continue, or piecing together the remnants of a dream you abandoned a long time ago, now is the time to start collecting your story. Start from the beginning of the challenge or obstacle. What were you attempting to accomplish? What was your original goal?

Write for Perspective

In addition to jogging your memory, the act of writing gives you perspective. In discussing the benefit of perspective, Richard Keith Latman of *Inc.* magazine says, "The skill is in getting up to 50,000 feet; above your issues, problems and opportunities, and being able to look down as objectively as possible to see if there is a path."[27]

On the written page, everything that you record, sits on neutral ground relative to everything else. There is no lens of judgment or criticism; you will have your opportunity for self-critique later. The paper gets to be a neutral observer of what you record. While you may feel like you're hardly making progress, or even moving backwards, the objective observer can help you see for yourself the reality in your experience of having drawn closer to your goal.

Inevitably, along the process of creating your accounting and collecting the details, ideas will arrive, along with judgments and the urge to self-critique. On a separate paper, or elsewhere in a notebook, keep those ideas and mental scraps. You'll be able to make use of them later. But, don't let them distract you and get in the way of you recording as much as you can. It doesn't have to be long or short, but should include as much detail a possible.

To recap, because having the accounting is such an important and therapeutic step in the process of Regrouping, I want to go over the reasons why we should pursue creating a record of our experience, both the internal and external one. This will help to frame how to go about it.

<u>First</u>, we want to be able to preserve as many of the details of our experience as possible. The mind has a natural tendency to forget over time.

<u>Second</u>, we want to provide a cathartic release of the feelings and thoughts that coincide with circumstances and events that we are confronting.

<u>Third</u>, we want to be clear about what we were hoping to accomplish and encapsulate as much as we can as guidance for later endeavors.

<u>Forth</u>, we want to be able to secure perspective and closure for the events that transpired. That means that we need to be able to process events and feelings as fully and completely as possible.

<u>Fifth</u>, we want to outsmart our mind to be able to clearly see the actual accomplishments and success that were achieved in spite of and along the way to a seemingly negative conclusion.

<u>Sixth</u>, we want to start the process of first forgiving, and then eventually, congratulating yourself.

Remember, a setback is just a challenge with the wrong outcome. If you keep going and try again, with new information and a new approach, you can learn to change the outcome.

Getting Started

To create your account and/or journal, you should not necessarily focus on length. You'll also want to avoid feeling overwhelmed by the idea of having to go back over what may be a lengthy period of time or a significant number of events if you have not been recording all along the way. If you just commit 10 minutes a day to writing, you'll be pleasantly surprised at how much progress can be made in a relatively short period of time.

To provide some ideas about how to start your journal, consider answering the following questions relating to the circumstance(s) responsible for your setback or obstacle:

What did you originally set out to do?

What most excited you about that objective?

What was the first thing that you tried along that pursuit?

What was the first obstacle that you faced?

What other significant obstacles did you face?

What moment made you feel the happiest along that path?

What moment made you feel the worst along that path?

What moment makes you laugh when you think about it?

What did you accomplish that you didn't think you could?

Which of your goals did you accomplish?

Which of your goals did you not accomplish?

If your memory has already started to erase some of the important details, which as science has shown us, the mind is wont to do, consider some of these following sources of memory prompts to help you remember:

Go through your old emails.

Review the old text messages and photographs stored in your phone.

Scroll through your Facebook/Instagram/Twitter or other social media feed.

Read through your old blog posts or journal entries.

Once you have your accounting, you can even take the extra step of creating a visual representation of your experience by drawing out the literal highs and lows across a timeline. It is a great exercise for those of us who like to see things beyond words, and would benefit by having a tangible or more salient and creative outlet beyond just writing.

Find the Lessons

Having created your accounting, which is an extraordinarily valuable repository of knowledge and experience, you can start mining it for your own lessons. Potentially, you already started forming those insights as you were writing. Carve out some time and space for yourself to read everything you've written from beginning to end with an open mind and without judgment. As I read through my own calamity journal, I was happily surprised by the insights that came rushing along in the process. I kept a piece of paper within reach to record these thoughts.

On the second read through, do so while considering some of these following questions. It may even be beneficial to make a copy of your journal so that you can use a highlighter to mark particularly important sections.

Consider:

What are some immediate ideas of what you would do differently?

What was missing in this adventure that you wish you had or would like to have next time (knowledge/expertise, resources, tools, money, team members, etc.)?

What were the 5 most difficult decisions that you faced?

Which of those decisions turned out to be right?

What result did you expect from that decision?

What, if anything, was different from your expectations?

Which of those decisions turned out to be wrong?

What result did you expect from that decision?

What was different from your expectations?

What did you want to try, but did not?

Why not?

What are three things that you did really well?

What was it that enabled you to do those things (e.g., education, prior experience, help from others, etc.)?

What are three things that you did not do well?

What was it that hindered your performance (e.g., lack of information/expertise, lack of resources, lack of time, etc.)?

What part of the experience are you happiest about?

What part of the experience do you regret most?

What was the best advice that you received? From whom?

Would it be possible and valuable to have that person advise you more substantively?

Imagine that someone considering pursuing the same objective that you did has come to you for advice. What are the top three things you would tell him/her? Why?

The 5 Whys

As you answer these questions for yourself, I want to introduce to you a technique called the "5 Whys." I didn't create it. Rather, it is one of the foundational elements of some of the most successful operational systems in the world. It was invented by the founder of what we know today as Toyota, the number eight company as ranked by *Fortune Magazine* for worldwide revenues.[28]

Kiichiro Toyoda is recognized as the founder of the Toyota automotive company. However, it was his father, Sakichi Toyoda, probably one of Japan's most famous inventors, who actually started the original company, Toyoda Loom Works Ltd. The elder Toyoda was a great contributor to the philosophies, insights and practices that became the famed Toyota Production System, which has set a standard for some of the most popular business practices that we know, including six sigma. Six sigma has been used for years to improve manufacturing processes, making them more efficient and less likely to produce errors.[29]

The idea behind the 5 Whys is to get to the root cause of a problem by forcing one to dig deeply beyond surface reasons. This is achieved by asking "why" at least five times in the course of examining the reason behind a failure.[30]

For example, let's say that my favorite sweater does not fit. *Well, why is that?* Either it doesn't fit because I got bigger, or it got smaller. Let's assume for the sake of my own ego, that it got smaller. *Why is that?* Let's say, it got smaller because it's made out of wool and was recently washed in hot water. Most people would stop their inquiry here—now we know that the wool sweater, which should be washed in cold water not to shrink, was instead washed in hot water. This is seemingly an obvious answer to why the sweater does not fit. But, as a very important distinction, central to the 5 Whys technique, this answer does not address the problem of how to ensure that *no more* sweaters are inadvertently shrunk because we have not yet gotten into the process to *fix the error*. So, with three more "whys" left, let's go back to the inquiry.

The sweater was made out of wool and was recently washed in hot water. *Why is that?* Because the clothes were not properly sorted. *Why is that?* Because there is only one clothing hamper rather than two. Why is that? I only had one clothing hamper, simply because I did not know that I needed another one and didn't buy one.

Can you see how taking a deeper dive leads to a solution that addresses not only the immediate circumstance, but also gives us a solution to implement that can fix the root of the problem?

What I appreciate most about this technique is the core assumption that each person is capable of solving the problems they face *if* they have the correct *process*. It provides a clear and immediate course of action that can be pursued to improve later outcomes for even the most challenging problems we face. And with these solutions, we are better able to learn our lessons and plan for the future.

It is most helpful to utilize the 5 Whys process on any specific problems that you identified while working through your accounting. These would probably be answers to the following types of questions:

What are the five most significant obstacles that you faced?

What was the obstacle that you could not move past?

What where the three biggest problems that went unsolved?

If you could name a problem or obstacle that directly resulted in the current setback or challenge, what would it be?

By framing up the right questions, this process will help you to explore the cause and effect relationships that underlie and ultimately lead you to the root cause of these significant problems.

You should also be aware of some of the most relevant critiques of the 5 Whys method, as this exposes its limitations. Some have said that the answers that you will be able to reach in asking the 5 Whys will be limited by your current knowledge and further, that some problems are too complex to be able to drill down to a single root cause.[31] Both of these are true. However, simply going through the process will shed light on the problem to the extent of your current knowledge and give you, if not the root cause, at least one or more factors that you can address as a point of learning.

As you work through the 5 Whys, make sure that you do not wind up with a root cause that is somehow based on human error or simple mistakes. Again, the key assumption is that *people are always capable if the right process is in place.* So, the 5 Whys is not the place for blaming yourself or others. It is to find a process that you can put in place to help eliminate the circumstances that cause errors to be made. While you may want to blame only yourself for certain outcomes, and not your actions objectively, it leaves you with less power to change the circumstances. While you might be limited in your ability to change yourself, you certainly can quickly change your actions and circumstances, especially with additional information. You can gain knowledge and expertise; you can make money; or, like me with the shrunken sweater, you can always buy a second clothing hamper. With your time and your freedom, virtually anything is possible—you just need to know what it is that needs to be done.

Forgiveness and Allowing

In addition to the self-critique inherent in a debrief, forgiveness and allowing are just as essential. I will talk about allowing first because, for most, it is often easier to stomach than forgiveness, which is its own challenge.

Allowing

Some, but not all, of my friends and family know that for a small period, as another of my side adventures, I decided to explore stand-up comedy. I thought that it would be cool if I could learn how to perform. Even if I never used it professionally, knowing how to make people laugh seemed like a nice skill to have and fun to develop. During this time, it couldn't have been more ironic that I was employed as an attorney at a very serious law firm. But, in my mind, that was only during the day.

Taking advantage of being in California, I had some time

prior decided to take acting lessons. I didn't know it then, but this small "rebellion" was part of trying to break through the box of other people's expectations for me and, of what I should be as a person, as a lawyer and as a professional. I wanted to explore. And I'm forever grateful that I did. I was extremely lucky in my choice of acting teachers – I happened upon Richard Lawson's class and to this day I am convinced that I learned from the very best. He is a noted actor in his own right, but also an extremely powerful positive force that ennobles artists to walk in their own strength and power everyday through his work. He also happens to be stepfather to Beyoncé, whose inspirational approach to challenges I discussed in chapter 1.

After Lawson's class, I realized that I needed to find additional freedom—to be more open and true to who I was and what I wanted to say. Having been trained as a lawyer, it is tough to shake the careful, measured and politically-correct approach to communication. Often, what we do professionally, and how we do it creeps over into how we behave even outside of the office. Recognizing this, my search for the truth within and for a purer expression of the words I wanted to speak led me to standup comedy—the barest and most exposed form of art I know.

In the course of introducing myself to a new craft, I spent a lot of time hanging around comics "backstage" at the comedy clubs. Actually, on many nights, with no major headliner show, there usually was no conventional backstage. There was only an area, usually somewhere near the bar, where the comics would hang out before and after they stepped up to the microphone. We'd talk and I got to know them, their cadence, and their way with words, just in a regular one-to-one way. Our conversations would always be substantive, and hilarious. Because, honestly, what is funnier that the rawest and most delicate truth?

"Success is always less funny than failure"
– Jon Ronson

Eventually, I started giving my own performances. I'd go to open mic nights and I even did a showcase with a full five minutes of my own material. With the burden of a demanding job and the double shift of late nights in the comedy clubs, I lasted about six months. It wasn't my passion, and so my desire for it wasn't strong enough to see it through past the difficulty. But, boy did I learn. Not only did I learn to stop overthinking everything I say and become a lot more naturally raw in communication, but I also saw something in that experience that has fundamentally shaped my understanding and view of failure.

Night after night, at the open mics, I'd see comics go up with pages and pages of material. They didn't have polished sets, and most of the time, they weren't even good – their delivery, or the jokes they were telling. Some, would even come up with a stack of note cards, and stand alone, in front of a microphone, harshly lit by the spotlight above and simply read the joke on one card and pause, waiting for the groans, the laughs, or the boos. And then, without hesitation, they'd read the next, and the next, and the next in the exact same way. Sometimes, my guts would churn and ache for them, because at first I didn't understand why someone would come to fail, and fail miserably at that. But then, eventually, I'd see that comic again – in fact, I saw many of them multiple times, including some of the names we see now on television and in the biggest movies. At times, they'd just be trying out material, but at other times, they were getting the laughs out of the room, more and more each time.

Watching, I learned that the boos didn't kill them. In fact, the comics had a secret weapon coming to the stage that actually made them kind of immune to the harshest criticism. That secret weapon? The ability and intention to improve. Those comics knew no matter what happened on that night, or on any other night, although they were there to entertain, that this booing audience, perched in the illusion of power and judgment on chairs like tiny individual thrones, had it all wrong. The comics knew that rather than them working for the audience, the audience was actually *working for them*. With rapt attention, there they were, eager to judge, but in truth, simply hoping to hear something from that microphone that would stir a place somewhere deep where our own truths are buried.

During the time she was on stage, as the audience, we were in the comic's control, whether we knew it, or not. Our reactions, boos that we might have thought would be discouraging with biting disapproval, for the best comics, fueled a relentless drive to get better. Our laughter, for us, mini celebrations of the collective reality that we all share, were just lights for the comic, illuminating the right path for her material. Because, truthfully, no matter what we, the audience, did that night, the comic was going to grow. She was going to reap the benefits because regardless of what happened when she performed, as long as she stepped on the stage even just *one more time* after that, she would have gained something.

I have always found comedy to be a beautiful art—even the forms to which I could not relate. After standup, I decided to explore a group-based form of comedy called Improv, a name which harkens to its roots in improvisation. The foundation of Improv is a philosophy called "*yes, and.*" Essentially, as a player in an Improv "game," or *Harold* as the scenes are called, no matter what happens before you act or speak, you must accept and allow it, hence the "*yes.*" And then you are to build upon what was said before your turn as if it was meant to happen exactly that way, which accounts for the "*and.*" This includes mistakes. For example, you could start a Harold with the topic of children's shoes and wind up minutes later in an imagined scene on Mars. Sometimes it was funny; sometimes it was almost funny, but all of the time it was freeing.

"I think one of the greatest gifts we can give ourselves is letting go of what other people think of us."

– Sara Blakely

In the real world, we do face certain consequences for our mistakes, but the truth is, they're usually not as bad as we make them out to be in our mind. This is especially true for earnest mistakes made when we truly set out to do the right thing. Allowing yourself the space to explore, to try out your "material" so to speak, gives you the incomparable ability to learn from your decisions *and* mistakes.

Forgiveness

Alongside allowing for mistakes and learning, you must forgive yourself and others. I had to learn the power of forgiveness and reinforce its necessity by seeing what it looks like when you don't practice it.

When one of my early professional adventures ended in what I experienced as betrayal and a deep personal disappointment, I was faced with what I felt to be an impossible task, forgiving the two people I felt were responsible for my discomfort. One of those people was me. I had to learn how to forgive myself.

Thrust into a sea of change and uncertainty, in the struggle for survival, to regain your footing and to catch your next breath, it may seem counter-intuitive to also be worried about forgiving others or yourself. At least, I felt that way. I felt that forgiveness was something that I could wait on, if I ever got around to it at all. The circumstances that I faced, the pain, the feeling of loss, was something that I never wanted to feel again. I wanted to put it in my rear view as quickly as possible.

I felt like the act of forgiving would be an unwitting endorsement of the person who had set out to harm me. If I didn't hold on in some way to the wrong that he did, somehow in the fabric of the universe, it would be forgotten—a reward he certainly did not deserve. In part, being unforgiving felt almost like my responsibility, an invisible duty that only I could meet. And while everyone else was bewitched by this person's charming personality, misstatements and seeming wit, I would be the one to hold on to the truth of who he really was. Moreover, because I had been the one to trust him in spite of my discomfort, I wanted to hold on to my guilt as well, so that I wouldn't ever forget, and make that same mistake again. Until I forgave, I could always yank on that invisible cord and feel its tug and be reassured that neither one of us, neither him, nor me would walk away free.

But what I didn't realize at the time was that moving on without forgiving is like driving away with a towline still connected to your bumper. It is the danger of moving on without moving through. As far away as you go, something will happen that can forever continue to pull you back—that is, until you release that situation. Forgiveness is release. It is not an endorsement of a negative outcome or bad action. It is a refusal to be bound by it.

Thankfully, even in the midst of the confusion and the undesirable experience that this person caused, in spite of my temporary uncertainty about what to do next, one thing was very clear – it was a ringing in my gut. In the face of my instinct to hold on, for all of the noble reasons I could name, I knew that I had to forgive as quickly and as fully as possible. At the very beginning, this mandate was so far beyond me – it was all I could do to turn it over repeatedly in my mind during my daily morning walks around my neighborhood. *Forgive? After what happened? After what he did?* Unthinkable. *How could I even begin to forgive him, or myself?* But, something happens after you spend some time asking yourself the same question over and over each day – a tiny spark of an answer does begin to form. Then, I realized that to forgive him, I had to be able to thank him for something, anything, coming from the experience. And it was on that day that I realized that forgiveness, even for the unforgivable, can begin with gratitude. It is an opening when you have no idea where else to start.

Gratitude

With that tiny spark, the very beginning of forgiveness, I started to think about what I was truly thankful for, irrespective of how it ended. And there was so much to name. First, it was a leap of faith that got me out of the stagnation of over-comfort. It broke an unnecessary attachment to a completed dream so that I could start creating and pursing new dreams. Second, it showed me what I was capable of accomplishing, even in the midst of challenging circumstances. Third, it brought me many wonderful friends and professional associates that I would have forever. Fourth, it taught me invaluable lessons, both personal and professional, that I would not have learned elsewhere; and, finally, it brought me a little closer to being unafraid to fail or fight for myself.

In spite of the pain of that situation, I wouldn't have traded it for anything. I might have done it differently if given the choice, but I would have still done it. With continued focus on gratitude, my mind's conversation changed from negative thoughts to a practice of "thank you." Not thank you for the adversity, but thank you for the *opportunity to grow*. Not only was this gratitude necessary to extend to others, but it was also necessary to extend to myself as well.

Years later, on a random day in New York, I ran into someone who brought me right back to this experience of gratitude and forgiveness. I don't even know for certain how we began our conversation, but as it turned out, she had experienced a similar circumstance and challenge with the same person that I had. She also felt hurt, betrayed and angry. The difference, however, between her and me at that time was that I had already forgiven and she had not. As we spoke openly, even as strangers, the unity created by a shared experience established a familiarity and bond that belied the fact that we had just met. And I noticed that even as we were discussing current challenges, seemingly unrelated to what happened so many years ago, there was a connection in her mind between her current misfortune and that one experience long ago - that one moment of betrayal by this person we had in common. For her, the release had not yet come. After sharing tears and stories, I let her into the most important part of my story, the one that my new friend was missing—forgiveness.

It wasn't easy, but over time, as we stayed in touch, I watched as she slowly grew out of the darkness that had lingered over her, rooted in an unfinished story whose last page she previously refused to read. She began going to spiritual services and embarking on new personal and professional creative projects. I watched as this person's star began to shine brightly once more. After a while apart, we spoke again and I could hear the lightness in her voice—and this time we spoke of our many blessings and our gratitude for each one. There was no more talk of the past, only excitement for the future. And I also knew, in that friendship, I had one more thing to be thankful for.

Change is hard. For many, forgiveness is harder. But, gratitude is easy and that is the first step. Beyond gratitude, another ingredient for forgiveness is hope. Rather than holding on to grudges against others, or guilt, which is a grudge you hold against yourself, decide instead to hold on to hope and the vision for what you'd still like to accomplish. Although forgiveness is a deeply personal process for each person, as you begin to fill your mental and emotional space with the positivity of gratitude and hope, you simultaneously push out the negativity of grudges and guilt.

Beyond guilt, you can choose to hold on to something else – something greater and more noble. Make it a cause worthy of your attention, of your new and improved self. Find something to help even more people, and move beyond the smallness of one bad person or a bad decision. Choose bigger and bolder. There will always be people who take advantage of others; there will always be mistakes that follow bad decisions; but as long as we maintain our focus and preserve our strength by letting go of what does not serve us, we can and will be the light in the darkness to mark the path of progress.

You might hold your own internally-justified reasons for not forgiving, even in spite of the fact that it will come at the cost of your other worthwhile efforts. Is it worth it? What is a more freeing path and pursuit that you could choose? Can you be grateful enough for the lessons that have strengthened you? Can you be hopeful enough about your plans for the future that you can then let go of your past and embrace what is to come?

Do yourself the favor of answering these questions before you finish your debrief:

> What are three things that you are thankful for that came from this experience?
>
> What are three things that you are glad you did in the con-

text of this experience?

What is one thing that you are proud of yourself for related to this experience?

What is one thing that you are not happy about from this experience that you are willing to let go of?

Give yourself the gift of gratitude each day for the blessings and gifts that come alongside the obstacles and setbacks. Forgiveness essentially means moving forward with the rewards reaped from your challenge. Your arms can only carry so much—if you're holding on to the negative, you don't have room to hold the positive. For that reason, let go of as much of the negative as you can, so that you can retain the lessons, the friendships, the experience and the courage gained from your own pursuits.

Debrief to Win

Undertaking the process of debriefing is valuable (and free) therapy in the midst of addressing a setback or challenge. It ensures that you're able to capture the fullest recollection possible, which includes the valuable lessons contained within. If you can't remember it, or don't have it recorded, you'll never be able to learn from it. That would be a partial waste of your hard-earned experiences. The elements of allowing, gratitude and forgiveness, give you the opportunity to release the damage and pain that would otherwise threaten to weigh you down and hold you back. Some of the most successful people in the world use this tool to their advantage—it keeps them optimistic, centered, and, as we learned, even helps them recover more quickly after a setback. It is truly a winning advantage.

Following a debrief, finding the lessons, and even forgiveness and gratitude are somewhat easier than finding cause for celebration, or the basis to congratulate yourself for the part of the experience that you did well. When you encounter a disappointing result, regardless of the effort put in, it is easy to overlook the victories along the way. We are usually excellent self-critics, sometimes far too good at this work. Gratitude and forgiveness are the earliest steps, but realizing the fullness of what you accomplished is oftentimes difficult to see on your own. For this reason, we need others to help us shine a bit of light on the reasons to pat ourselves on the back. The process of a Regroup isn't all heavy and difficult self-analysis, some of it is enjoyment. In the next chapter, I'm going to introduce you to the people who will be your cheerleading section, whether you want one or not. Prepare to meet your "Forceful Congratulators."

Chapter 5:
Rely on "Forceful Congratulators"

A "Forceful Congratulator" may sound like a non-sequitur and in some ways, the actual person is as unique and unusual as the title. Many of us, taught to be achievers, are raised from childhood within a system that clearly rewards *winning* and punishes *losing*. This system has entrenched in us a very binary way of looking at ourselves. We get *grades* and we are hired, or fired—we graduate or we don't; we *fail* or *succeed*. And all of this means something pretty definitive when it comes to considering the options available to us for our future. Because the consequences are entrenched at such an early age, we internalize the teacher, the critic, and the measurement to make sure that we always make the mark and never fall below it. But, what we do not learn to do is congratulate ourselves for a job not well-done, but a job half-done.

If we miss the mark of our goals and objectives, we are not likely to throw ourselves an "almost, but not quite" party to celebrate our accomplishments. In fact, if someone did this on our behalf, we'd probably become offended and march out. Most of us do not want false praise.

False praise is not useful along the path of learning, growth and progress. It can do the job of temporarily bolstering our damaged egos, but not the real work of building actual confidence in ourselves and our capabilities. This aside, even when we do not make it all the way to our goal, we still need to recover and recognize what was actually achieved in the attempt. This type of congratulations is not a replacement for the rewards of a goal met, nor should it erase your goal or substitute your drive to accomplish that goal. It should not completely eliminate the itch of discomfort from knowing that something you badly want still eludes you.

What we want to avoid, is the discomfort becoming so heavy, so unnecessarily thick that we are unable to see the breadcrumbs of success that we earned along the way. A little bit of discomfort is good; too much can be destructive. To balance, false praise is also unwanted, as it threatens to prematurely remove our discomfort and lull us into complacency. Yet, for some of us, the resistance to *any* praise is so strong that a truly forceful voice, from someone that you not only trust, but who is credible, informed and insistent, can often be the only way to make us realize our smaller accomplishments. This person helps us find perspective and validates the key rewards of this stage of the journey so far. This person is your "Forceful Congratulator."

The First "Forceful Congratulator"

A forceful congratulator is a person who insists that you recognize your accomplishments, even in the midst of what you're experiencing as a failure. They will twist your arm to make you pat yourself on the back.

This term came up for me because of my father. Following my experience with QVC, I was so disappointed with myself that I didn't get a chance to tell the entire wonderful story of the product that I was presenting. I felt like I had blown our big chance, because I wasn't able to say everything that I had planned. I had watched the movie *Joy* and I just believed entirely that it was my responsibility to sell out of our complete stock on our first airing. Anything short of that, in my mind, was a complete and utter failure.

After the airing, I was definitely demonstrating my disappointment. I wasn't myself and it showed. I spoke about it over and over to anyone who would listen. Finally, it was my Dad, who said to me, "Are you crazy? You sold hundreds! In just 7 and a half minutes on your first time! Somebody heard you – maybe you didn't get to say everything, but you said enough. You did great!" And you would have to know my Dad to know that he doesn't mince words. He's very much a matter-of-fact person, accustomed to informing people of the reality and gravity of their circumstances. For example, when I graduated from Harvard Law School and I asked him if he was proud, he told me, "I paid for years of private school and for Duke, this is what I expected of you." There was never any room for false praise.

So, his passionate appeal when speaking about QVC definitely took me by surprise. I expected him to have the same perspective as I did, that I could have and should have done better, leaving me no space to accept less than my absolute best. But instead, he was just so passionate about a different perspective, I remember thinking it was almost like we were having a disagreement. I definitely realized that I needed to pay attention.

This is where the "forceful" aspect originated. It was this strong counterbalance to the swarming storm of self-critique that brewed in my mind. But, *forceful* is what it took for his voice to break through the internal dialogue that was starting to cloud my perspective of my experience. The key is that he did more than just say "congratulations" or "you did a great job." It is very hard to hear praise or congratulations for something I know I could have done better. In my mind, by identifying the faults, I ensure that I don't make those same mistakes in the future. However, by skipping over the successes, I also have no idea of the map that I've been creating all along the way. The complement to learning what doesn't work is learning what does. It may not be enough to get you all the way there, but it's more than what you started with. To use it, you have to be able to see it.

Insistent and Earnest

In the midst of a setback, swimming in the stinging pain of disappointment and self-critique, a forceful congratulator is not just about making you feel better as quickly as possible, it is much more honest. To be effective, the process takes a little more time, a little more intention and has some passion behind it. It really takes an insistent approach—someone who sets out to make sure that you hear and internalize the identification of your wins in the midst of what you may feel like has missed the mark.

Find Your Forceful Congratulator

Finding your own forceful congratulator will help you to start to rise above the internal and external noise that tries to invalidate your accomplishments. Though my father was my first forceful congratulator, I've started to identify more forceful congratulators in my life. I now rely on my mother and other family, certain friends, my partner, and my mentors to guide me through a setback with my hard-earned accomplishments acknowledged.

As I've observed in myself and many others, people most successfully internalize the critic, but almost never internalize the congratulator. Forceful congratulators play that role of making sure that you recognize your true gains along the way, however small. This helps to mark that you are en route and making progress. While you're focused on the end goal that may be so far away, and you've already made a big push that doesn't get you all the way there, it can feel like you're standing still, or even moving backwards. Enter the wonderful forceful congratulator. They don't just tell you "nice try" or "good job" and move on – they make an actual personal investment in getting past the noise in your mind to make sure that you hear, see and can identify for yourself *what exactly was the good job* and why you should feel some sense of accomplishment in the midst of self-critique or self-doubt.

The Role of Mentors and Sponsors

Mentors and sponsors can play the role of a forceful congratulator for you from time to time, but not necessarily all the time. A mentor or sponsor gives you the benefit of experience and access to help identify and pursue your best next step. They can shed light on your map or be a compass to help understand where you actually are along your journey. Sometimes, a mentor can also be a forceful congratulator—their experience gives them enough perspective to see your win or progress along an uncertain path or not-yet-reached success. Having a mentor or sponsor who can say "I've been there" or "I've seen that before" and then from a place of authority also add "It's not as bad as you think" or "Here's the good to be found in this situation" winds up serving a dual role.

Still, a forceful congratulator can be anyone with credibility in your eyes, who has some knowledge of the situation and can contribute perspective for the positive, intentionally and unrelentingly. The mentor can do so from her position of authority, but one doesn't rule out the other. The forceful congratulator's role is to give focus and power to the positive that is being overlooked—to give you a more realistic perspective.

A Work in Progress

With a shift in perspective, a setback or failure becomes a partial success. With a renewed intention to continue, a partial success then becomes an incomplete success. With unrelenting pursuit of the goal, eventually an incomplete success reaches its intended final destination. Going back to my QVC example, once I was able to make the shift in perspective to viewing my experience as a partial success, I started pulling lessons out of it in preparation for my next airing, with a renewed attitude of excitement. I felt with one airing under my belt, I could really nail it the next time. And even if I were to present a different product or even on a different platform, what I learned about how to present information to those that want it (and how not to), is something that I got to take away as a present that I earned for myself. Thankfully, it was a gift that I didn't simply throw away because the eventual outcome was a little different from my original intentions. And if you're wondering how it all worked out, the brand was invited back just months later for another appearance, affording the chance to build on what it turns out, was a great start.

Why You Should Become a Forceful Congratulator for Others

Should you decide that you want to become a forceful con-gratulator for others (and you should), it will require you to be three things: *honest*, *informed* and *convincing*. You are literal-ly going to be the opposing force to a very potent, seemingly all-knowing, and very persuasive presence inside the mind of your friend, partner, or loved one. The job of their internal voice is to echo the doubts, concerns and rationale that would speak *against* the pursuit of their dreams and aspirations - in essence, anything potentially worthwhile, but with an uncertain outcome. Once that voice is emboldened by an opening created by a setback or obstacle, it looks for any fuel it can find, via social media, news programs and even misinterpretations of seemingly unrelated information, to discourage its target. Even worse, that voice is a constant presence – always there, doing its work.

As a person who believes in your friend, colleague, child or whoever it is that you are encouraging, you see their struggle, you admire their courage and strength to embark upon something that they envisioned for themselves, breaking from the safety of stagnation and complacency. You find them inspiring. As an outsider, you can see all of the progress that they have made—you remember where they started and it's been a marvelous thing to watch. In fact, if you're honest, you can't even believe that they've made it this far.

So, when they stumble, you want more than anything to see

them continue. You don't want them to be hurt. You want them to be happy and fulfilled. And you could swear you saw them happy—many moments along the way, even if this particular setback has got them down. You know that if they just keep going, they could do it; they could reach their goal. So, you listen more closely to what he or she is telling you, and spend a few minutes doing your own research. You take the time to get informed. The next time you speak, you'll be able to provide specific details that will lend perspective. Perhaps they'll listen. If not, you'll try again, because it matters, they matter. And each time, you learn a little more, try a different angle, always being honest and pushing a little bit more against their wall of self-doubt.

Eventually, he hears you, she hears you. And you've helped save a dream, and as a bonus, you get to feel uplifted as you see another setback surmounted.

It always is helpful to sit on the opposing side of your own situation. It allows you to see your circumstances more clearly. You should practice being a forceful congratulator for others because first, it allows you to start to see the self-talk that happens for all of us, and how much it can distort reality. Second, it is a great bonding exercise and helps to build and strengthen your tribe. Third, you'll pick up lessons along the way, gaining expertise in other areas that might inform your own journey.

To become a better forceful congratulator for a person that you value, you could work on improving your credibility, by, for example listening more closely to how the process is unfolding for them, or learning a bit more about the endeavor that your friend, partner or even child is pursuing, so that the congratulations you give are more specific.

You can also work on focusing your intent in providing congratulations, not just to say something in an attempt at a "feel good moment." Instead, drive to create an *understanding* in that person. It is completely different from how we view normal or traditional congratulations, which tend to be non-specific and don't really fully take into account the journey along the way. In this type of congratulations, the *journey* is the focus.

A long time ago, we used to all be explorers and there was nothing to be made but mistakes along the way to our greatest inventions, discoveries and implementations that have contributed to our way of life today. Our biggest rewards and accolades still go to the rare breed of inventors and explorers who find a way out of established and default thinking to seek out the answers to lingering questions. Will you be next?

An Incredibly Successful "Failure"

To see the effects of forceful congratulations, consider the path of Sara Blakely, the creator of Spanx. As a child, growing up, her father would regularly ask Blakely and her brother "what did you fail at this week?"[32] In doing so, he fostered a spirit of exploration, instilling an expectation of not just pushing the limits, but of trying again, undaunted by the internal or external judgments of a missed mark. Blakely used this training to surmount the many obstacles that she faced in establishing the Spanx brand – going from just a simple idea to an incredibly successful business.

To hear her tell it, Sara was never particularly good at any particular thing. In fact, in the pursuit of her dream to follow in the steps of her father, an attorney, she "failed" the LSAT twice, essentially foreclosing the avenue of law school, in favor of other, less traditional endeavors. Her first job, as short-lived as it was, found her at Disney World, again, falling "short" so to speak, as her 5'6" height prevented her from taking her preferred role of playing Goofy. She needed to be two inches taller to fit into the costume. She next took a job selling fax machines, in an entry-level position that would max out for her at $40,000 per year.[33] Today, Blakely, comfortably resides on the list of the world's richest people, having entered the *Forbes* list as the young-est self-made billionaire in 2012.[34] If you hear her story, you'll see how the role of the forceful congratulator can be credited for setting the foundation of her success.

In many interviews, Blakely consistently tells the story of her father's encouragement to fail at something, anything. After posing his regular question at the dinner table, "what did you fail at this week?", if she did not have an answer, her father would be disappointed. But, if she did have an answer, like a terrible try out for example, he would be the first to offer a high five and a "way to go!" He would ask for details and show his interest in the story, to emphasize the weight of the *experience*, which was the jewel in their conversation, rather than the final result.[35]

This is the essence of a forceful congratulator. Their job is to reframe your thinking, to pull out of your experience the gems that you've earned so that you have a clear perspective on the value of your efforts. As Sara Blakely characterized it, this "gift," was helpful to move the definition of failure away from the emphasis on a fixed end result and instead to define failure as the opportunities, lessons and experiences missed from never having tried at all.

It made Blakely fearless and allowed for a freedom to try— not to fail, but to fly.

Further into his role as an early forceful congratulator, Blakely's father forced her and her brother to *befriend* failure, by writing what they gained out of each moment when they did fail or miss an intended outcome. In an interview with *Success* magazine, of the experience, Blakely said, "You would realize like, *oh well, I didn't make the team, but I met my best friend in tryouts.* There was just always something there that made it worth doing."[36] She even has made a practice of finding the humor in the mess-up that forms the foundation of a story to entertain others. She says, "Oftentimes when things don't go well, I'm able to laugh at myself and turn it into a story. I like the art of storytelling, and my favorite part of the screw-up is being able to potentially make somebody else laugh or smile about it. It makes it all worth it."[37]

Blakely's humor and healthy attitude shines into her relation-ship with her husband. She's told the story of a cocktail party she attended where she was asked her life motto. Just as she was pre-paring to grace the eager ears with a dose of valuable wisdom, she realized that it had vanished from her mind. She simply couldn't recall her own motto for living. Her husband who had witnessed the moment, found it so funny that he turned her un-motto into its own iconic embodiment, creating a glass neon sculpture for a wall in their home that read, "I have a motto I live by but I forgot it."[38]

Having a father who was a forceful congratulator ingrained a creative and fearless approach to the endeavors that Sara would later undertake and also gave her the freedom to follow through on her vision for the product that the entire world would eventu-ally know as Spanx.

A forceful congratulator does not have to be just your father, or a mentor. It can be a friend, or a spouse, or coworker, or even someone that you just met. The most important qualities are: first, this person honestly believes in you; second, they refuse to give power to the idea of failure as a negative and final label on your attempt; third, they will force you to find the foundation of good in every experience, which will lead you to the gratitude, lessons and value to be found, no matter how things turned out; and finally, they should be credible—someone that you look up to and trust, with your best interests at heart and with some working knowledge of the situation at hand.

Some Thoughts Especially for Women and Girls

Sara Blakely's story is encouraging and unusual, not just because of the level of success that she's attained. Girls and the women we grow into tend to need forceful congratulators more than men. From what I've observed, *we*, myself included, sometimes internalize failure more often and more deeply. In terms of self-talk, we speak a different language. Whereas it seems that our male counterparts are more adept at finding an external attribution for shortcomings, women, we tend to blame ourselves and be less forgiving of our own mistakes. Perhaps, the world around us is also less forgiving of our mistakes as well. The need to prove ourselves becomes a persistent habit and distraction. So, as a woman, to have someone who can break through what can be louder noise, the defeating self-talk, is invaluable. This doesn't mean that men don't need a forceful congratulator, because they certainly do, but women might need one more often to balance our apparent inclinations.

At the risk of a generalization, I do believe that men are naturally more boastful, perhaps in some way conditioned to be so, and therefore are accustomed to taking credit as well as seeking and accepting praise more frequently. I've seen many (not all) men very skillfully take a small success and magnify it to appear like a much larger one. As a further generalization, women tend to be less natural self-promoters. So, to even acknowledge something as a success, for a woman, usually, we would have to feel like we've made a much bigger accomplishment to move the needle. And even in that circumstance, we gravitate more towards being a part of the background of doing the work and less about the lonely foreground in running a victory lap.

One way for women to change this inclination is to be the person for another that promotes their successes aloud. Be their ad hoc publicist. Simply hearing about your accomplishments from another not only makes you value those accomplishments more, but also teaches us how to phrase them in a way that is valuable information to others. If we hear you value them, then we learn to place our own value there as well. And I believe that it can be a beginning in helping to make us, as women and the girls on their way, more comfortable in moving the measuring post to recognize more of our accomplishments in the face of self-judgment.

Avoiding Distance

There is something more than the self-critic that discourages us from self-celebration. Even in the instance of accomplishing something noteworthy, I hesitate to name my successes because doing so feels to me like I am creating unwanted distance between myself and those that I want to connect to in communicating. Sometimes, I wonder if my accomplishment is even significant enough to warrant sharing it with others.

In the space of forceful congratulations, we allow ourselves permission to have our accomplishments amplified, so that we are forced to see and acknowledge them. In turn, we do the same for others. We create a safe space to be celebrated, free from the judgment of whether or not we're good enough, or have achieved enough while still being on our way to success. As an added bonus, it brings us closer together.

One day, perhaps, with enough practice, or a critical shift in how we measure ourselves, the forceful congratulator will become part of your internal dialogue. With the help of others, as you learn to identify and amplify your progress, you'll draw strength and inspiration from the encouragement of knowing you're moving forward along your intended path. What first appeared as a setback, becomes a circumstance that resulted in a valuable lesson to be used further down the road. What was previously discouraging gives way to a faint glimmer of hope in knowing that you have lost nothing, wasted little and have something to show for it after all.

Armed with the powerful ally of a forceful congratulator, you have the help that you need to extract the fullest value of the lessons that you've learned, which should reassure you that there is a way forward. And the choice of continuing upon your path is up to you. Even though the road is challenging and uncertain, you get to make your own choice of how to continue.

Protect Your Dreams from "Forceful Discouragers"

Just like there are people who will encourage you as forceful congratulators, there are also others, many times those who love you equally, who I call "Forceful Discouragers."

Forceful discouragers are people with limited visions because of their experiences and expectations. When you tell them that you plan to take a risk on something that they do not know or believe to be possible, if they can't see it, and especially if they care about you, they will fight tooth and nail to "protect" you from going down that road. To you, it will feel awful, as if you're not being supported.

Every word that echoes your inner doubts will feel like a sword piercing right through the center of your soul. It can feel like the very wind is being vacuumed out of your sails, just as you had developed enough courage to proceed against the tide. Just remember, inasmuch as your own mind is trying to protect you from expending energy, these people, the forceful discouragers, are simply doing their best to protect you from what *they* see as a potentially injurious path. They don't want you to expend resources chasing after an uncertain future. But they also don't see your truth and cannot look through your eyes into the future that you envision.

Avoid conversations about your dreams and plans with people who are forceful discouragers. They mean well, but unfortunately do more harm than good at a time when you need encouragement more than ever. Your dreams are as fragile as the wings of a newly-emerged butterfly. Protect and guard them with your silence as necessary.

This does not mean that anything that does not wholeheartedly endorse your plan or perspective as you see it should be ignored and discarded. But there is a time, place and manner for constructive criticism. In the early stages, when you're recovering from a setback, or have not yet developed your new plan to the stage where it's strong enough to be ready for the slings and arrows of critique, forceful discouragers are detrimental to your process of Regrouping. Focus on finding forceful congratulators instead, and let them help you win the battle against your obstacles.

Now that we've explored an entire universe of options to continue, in the next chapter, we'll explore the concept of "quitting" as a deliberate, informed decision and how that can also help you never completely give up.

REFOCUS

Chapter 6:
How to Quit Without Giving Up

S o far, I've spent this entire book encouraging you to stick with it, whatever "it" happens to be, no matter what. Now comes the time that we couple the pepper with the salt. You've been prepared with the right attitude, and know that you always have an opportunity to persevere. So, now, the coast is clear to give you some additional options.

The truth is, every attempt is not going to be the winning shot. Given unlimited time, resources and energy, you can accomplish absolutely anything you set out to do, even without finding the optimal way to get there. That said, and this is very important, we do not have unlimited time, resources or energy. Whatever we choose to put our efforts toward will necessarily take away from something else that we could also pursue. For this reason, our minds, similar to our bodies, are always taking us through the "*is it worth it?*" exercise, forcing us to constantly evaluate the cost of any effort we exert. In fact, it is often that "*is it worth it?*" question that derails us from an otherwise worthwhile pursuit because the weight of that question combined with any doubts lingering in our minds can often be too heavy to bear. As a result, we drop some of our best ideas and efforts because that single shred of doubt becomes magnified by the normal course of questioning in our own minds.

It is important not to let your ambitions, projects and plans come to a premature end. It is critical that you do not let the weight of doubt, whether magnified or not, convince you to turn a setback into a full-scale permanent stop. Coupled with that understanding, the reality is that some *projects* you attempt should at some point come to a conclusion, even before your actual goal is met. For whatever the reason, the *attempt* will be incomplete; perhaps due to missing resources, like time, money, knowledge, or even physical or emotional energy. An incomplete attempt does not mean a final end to an incomplete goal, dream or ambition. It just means that it may be time for you to pause, gather yourself, let the emotions come and pass, so that you can heal and start again with an improved plan.

In this chapter, we will discuss how you can quit, without ever giving up.

Preempting Failure

Our greatest champions are celebrated when they persevere to some point of natural completion. We find inspiration in movies like *300* which is a dramatization of the legend of the Battle of Thermopylae, from the times of Ancient Greece. This story has become such an iconic tale that it is rendered in innumerable forms of media beyond film, such as songs, poems, video games and even graphic novels. We are in love with the heroic idea of fighting until the end—not accepting defeat until you have attempted a trade of everything else of value. This is the hero's tale.

In far less extreme circumstances, when it comes to our own lives, we are much quicker to disembark, far before the ship hits the iceberg and well ahead of any true signs of trouble. Stories such as that of the captain going down with the ship or, the last place runner valiantly finishing the race, are our gold standard of courage, but we often fall short of this even with the most benign of pursuits. We are more inclined to throw hands in the air and offer "I quit" almost as some kind of counter-attack on the very effort that is kicking us toward defeat.

What is it that is gained on the way to failure? What seasoning comes as one draws closer to the flames of being defeated? It's something that we need to find out for ourselves more frequently. But, *how?* One of my favorite books on resilience, Grit by Angela Duckworth offers a simple solution, echoed by coaches, business leaders and even Duckworth's own parenting style. This simple advice is to *"never quit on your worst day."*[39] And while it would seem that your worst day would intuitively be the appropriate day to quit, from my own experience, I can agree that it is certainly not.

Duckworth advises that you should only quit upon a natural stopping point, such as the end of a series of classes, or the end of a sports season. But what about when your endeavor is not a limited or fixed type of engagement? How do you make your own determination when to quit if it is not at the moment when with every fiber of your being, you just want the discomfort to end? Duckworth, and coincidentally, every single trainer that I have ever worked with in the gym, all counsel that the moment of your greatest discomfort is exactly the point when you should *not* quit. Just as the point of pain is to signal that some real muscle work is about to happen, your discomfort signals that you have reached the horizon of where your own growth can now happen. No discomfort, no growth. No growth, no transformation.

So, other than becoming comfortable being uncomfortable, how do we go about finding a way to manage the many times extremely painful discomfort that can at times feel like its own death?

The Gift and Power of Vulnerability

I want to go back to telling you about my own experience with Cosmedicine. As part of my role as CEO, I had the accountability of having to present a progress report on our business to my board (i.e., my investors), each quarter. At the beginning, in re-launching the business, before the rubber ever hit the road, presentations were something that I looked forward to. They were simple updates and projections that were crafted in a perfect world and would continue to exist there until we launched. And when we did launch, we exceeded expectations with early wins and congratulations all around. Then, as the months progressed of our first year in operation, those quarterly meetings became much less enjoyable. The stress of having to explain the unforeseen obstacles that presented themselves was overwhelming to me, as a perfectionist. Further, the constant inundation on social media and other platforms of absolutely nothing but what seemed like stories of instant success had a compounding negative effect.

Eventually, my wonderful dream of a project started to feel like an actual job – the thing that I loved to do, started dragging on me and began to feel like work, especially when those quarterly meetings came around. I began to wonder, "is it worth it?" I managed to navigate the feelings of discomfort and unhappiness, but couldn't help but notice the thoughts regularly creeping into my mind to call it quits. But, although I wanted to quit, with a deep desire some days, I did not – I could not because I honestly and truly wanted more than anything else, to see it through.

Feeling wed to my circumstances, I began to see the effects of the mounting stress in my body. It was nothing that meditation, yoga, or running could fix. Instead, I needed a shift in perspective. Thankfully, on one weekend, prior to a quarterly meeting, the moment when my stress would typically be at maximum flux, I met up with some of my girlfriends for brunch. Where we typically all have a predictable auto-answer to "how are you?" that starts with either "good!" or "great!" one of us, gave the rare and unexpected gift of the truth. She said, "well, actually, today I am pretty sad." And immediately, we all rushed to comfort because that is what we all do—assuming something drastic anytime anyone steps out of the pseudo-happy convention that we've all become accustomed to. But, she did not want comfort, she was simply expressing her true feelings. And what we had just witnessed was a rare and unselfish act of pure vulnerability, allowing us into her truth as she was experiencing it – we got to see the magic of an incomplete experience, a work in progress, a success that she was still figuring out.

That morning my friend was working through the process of deciding to fold her own startup. Not because it was imminently failing, not because they had run out of money or would run out of money and not because the product was a bad idea. It was simply that her reasons for starting the company had not been fulfilled in the process of building it. And, with some experience running the business and a working knowledge of the path to meeting the company objectives, she knew what it would take to bring this idea to fruition. She understood and knew she *could* do it, if she wanted to; she knew *how* to do it – but she also knew that she just did not want to do it. And that is a powerful thing to know.

Her vulnerability allowed me to observe the process of how to decide to quit without actually giving up—how not to be controlled by circumstances or taken hostage by your emotions, dictating to you when you give up and cry "uncle." This was something new, a logical process that factored in unhappiness but made an *independent decision*, not based on emotion, but based on considering the same goal that sparked the experience at the beginning. It was a measuring post – a way to evaluate the experience that insured a transfer of the full wisdom and transformation to be gained, without succumbing to the destructive element of powerlessness.

I watched how quitting could actually become a practical tool in the battle for your dreams. When you make it a choice, on your terms, not swayed by the craving for relief, there is something to be won from making a decision to quit. To leave the battle for another day, another strategy, or even, for another person.

Looking back over the now innumerable times I *wanted* to quit, when I felt like yielding to discomfort and taking the cheapest and easiest exit to find relief, I realize that when things don't go as planned, the pain and the sharp and needling vice grip of unhappiness, will always come. And when it does, I will always want to be free of it, as quickly as possible – almost as urgently as if I were holding on to a hot bulb, freshly burned out from having been left on too long. I will always be tempted to let go of my dream – to drop it where it may shatter as a way to salvage my spirit. I have learned to respect that feeling, to allow it, but to not be governed by it. No matter how it *feels*, I have had to find a path to reinterpret what that uncomfortable feeling *actually* means – not that I am facing death, or my certain destruction, but that I am at the door of transformation and no matter what, I must walk through.

In these moments, I have taken to asking myself, "*If I give up, what does that look like?*" This means, aside from the discomfort that I feel, identifying which of the current tasks in front of me, is actually impossible. If not impossible, which is overly burdensome or just beyond my reach? If not burdensome, what is there on *today's* list to do that cannot be done?

On any given day, when you consider *only* that which must be done *immediately*, you will see that the idea of giving up in that moment, just when you feel like it, translates in practice to electing not to do something very simple that was of no real burden whatsoever. Now, whether it becomes a waste of time, or doesn't help accomplish a goal is a question to consider separately.

As for the discomfort that you feel, ask yourself, can it be managed another way?

"Courage doesn't always roar. Sometimes courage is the quiet voice at the end of the day saying, 'I will try again tomorrow.'"

– Mary Anne Radmacher

Before I give you options for how to quit, to save yourself from giving up, I want to talk more about discomfort. It comes for a reason – the ringing pain, it is something that can be moved through, but it is an appropriate warning of impending threat. Just like lifting weights in the gym creates tears in your muscles, these small injuries allow you to become stronger. These happen to be injuries that we want, but they are still injuries that our bodies and mind, through pain, work to prevent.

The same is true of discomfort following a disappointment or impending defeat. It is a pain that alerts you to a potential threat or problem. The feeling and the problem are not imagined, they are very real. In the past, whenever I took a professionally *adventurous* path, my greatest moments of discomfort came in form of a threat to my financial stability. For other people, their triggers may be shame, or something else that affects their sense of safety.

In learning how to manage discomfort, I have had to learn how to acknowledge, explore and address the feeling and find what concern it was pointing me to. If the potential threat was financial, I learned to create a realistic budget and start saving. If the potential threat was some other fault in the circumstances, I have learned to identify and address it. And if it couldn't be ad-

159

dressed, I used it as something that could and should inform my decision of *if*, not when, I should decide to quit. Besides pointing to the threshold of transformation, marking unchartered territory and a new frontier of growth, discomfort also indicates that something is unfamiliar, that it doesn't quite work and that the current path, if unchanged could lead to further problems down the road.

Before we explore making the decision about when to quit and how to quit, it's important to know *if* you should quit. And that is what discomfort is for— informing your decision of *if* you should quit. Discomfort is a counselor, a forceful suggestion that is an over-protective guidance. You have the choice and always will – the ifs, hows and whens, of your decision to quit, or stay in the ring, should be fully and completely up to you.

To productively engage with discomfort, similar to portions of the process in the debrief, it is easier if you unpack what you are experiencing. My way of doing that is to focus on answering simple questions. Next time you are experiencing discomfort, consider trying this exercise:

> List your concerns in this moment.
>
> Which of the concerns that you listed will definitely take effect today? Tomorrow?
>
> To meet your needs and perform your tasks for today, what resources are missing that would prevent you doing so?

To meet your needs and perform your tasks for a week from now, what resources are missing that would prevent you from doing so?

To meet your needs and perform your tasks a month from now, what resources are missing that would prevent you from doing so?

Of the concerns that you listed, which can you not address using readily available resources (knowledge, time, cash, energy, contacts, etc.,)?

Of the concerns that you listed, which will persist, no matter how you apply the resources that you currently have available?

Of these concerns, how does each impact your current activity? Do you expect that it will force you to stop, either today or in the near future?

Will this concern force you to stop in the next couple of months? Do you foresee any new resources becoming available during that time?

Today not being an option, when is the next stopping point that would arrive on its own, or without you causing it? (e.g., a point in which an external event, could influence your decision to quit.)

Assuming that you do decide to "quit," what does that entail, and what do you imagine that the next moment will be like? The next day? The next month?

Not giving up at the moment that you feel most uncomfortable is critical to ensuring that you'll grasp all the lessons you'll need to move forward later. In the times that felt like I was confronting the "impossible," my strong sense of commitment and my connection to my goal kept me going. But realistically, for me, you and everyone else, sometimes it is just not possible to move forward in the moment. Sometimes you are missing critical resources without which you truly cannot progress, and it will be helpful to explore some of the options for those times.

The Pause

When you hit a minefield of unexpected setbacks and obstacles in the process of working toward your goal, or completing a project, it is normal to feel overwhelmed, out of control and even powerless. These feelings can be debilitating. Even though caused by temporary circumstances, this kind of experience can be a significant factor in wanting to give up. You're exhausted, you've tried everything you can think of up to this point, and you just want a break from it all.

Give Yourself a Break

When an objective or goal looms ahead, it is natural to think of achievement as one strong push forward—with the belief that the same momentum that got you started will be the same momentum that you finish with. Usually, this is not the case.

"The size of your success is measured by the strength of your desire; the size of your dream; and how you handle disappointment along the way."

– Robert Kiyosaki

In any daring pursuit, there will come an inevitable moment when the task outmatches your skill, wit, resources and possibly even energy. Throughout this book, you have learned how to manage the way you interpret this moment. But, now what should you do? To Regroup in this moment means simply giving yourself a break. Temporally give it up, and just, for a precious few moments, lift off all of the weight of your struggle and relax. When you hit a wall, the best approach is not just to plow through it; it is to take a step back for a pause to gain perspective.

Giving yourself a break doesn't need to be a long and intense effort. There are many shortcuts and 'cheats' to provide a quick reset. Sleep is an incredible tool for resetting, as is exercise.[40] In a study published by Emily Bernstein, a Harvard University researcher, participants had an easier time managing their emotions in a controlled experiment, following a period of moderate aerobic exercise.[41] You can literally walk right into a new attitude.

Whichever path or method you choose, the most important thing is to give yourself permission to pause. Burning out is a completely avoidable end to an otherwise worthy endeavor. And believe me, I certainly wish that I had this advice on hand in some of my earliest pursuits.

The key to the pause is that you make an agreement with yourself in advance about how long your break will last, and that you keep to that agreement. If you plan to take a two-hour nap to reset, then set an alarm and make a commitment that it will be only two-hours. If you decide to come back to it tomorrow, actually start again tomorrow. To make the most of the opportunity to quit temporarily, and not let it lapse into giving up, you do have to make the commitment to continue. If you've done all of the prior work of being focused on your purpose, managing your self-talk, and finding the gratitude and lessons of your experience in your debrief, it should not be as big of a leap. It is a small step to take, but if you had the courage to start, you can find the courage to continue. You're stronger than you know and capable of far more than you give yourself credit for. *You have the tools to confront the obstacles and the attitude to meet success.*

Taking a pause is a tool that I use often to make my way through uncertain times, especially with the large obstacles that come my way. Let us recall my moment of melting to the floor (*gracefully*, though) when we had to change our packaging for QVC. In fact, now, I don't even wait to get to the point of feeling completely overwhelmed. If I see that I've come up against a setback, my first reaction is to say "ok." And I simply step away. I leave it there and accept it for what it is. I allow and honor the moment of pause. Even if I do not have the solution in the moment, or the right answer, I've grown comfortable in knowing that eventually, it will come—if I keep working on it. It's the step before my contingency plan, before I ask "if it weren't impossible…"

Sometimes, all you need is a solid pause and you can find your way back to a new set of options ahead of you. In other times, after you've stepped away and tried applying a new approach and a new perspective, the obstacle remains stubborn, or the circumstances remain unfavorable, and you'll need to pick a new direction. That is the realm of the pivot.

The Pivot

For entrepreneurs, the word "pivot" is rooted in the concept that the original idea that founders of a company started with is rarely the idea that they go to market with, or find ultimate success with. Have you heard of the company named Odeo, founded by Evan Williams and Biz Stone? Likely not, because Odeo, launched in 2005, was the original concept of the company that became what is known today as Twitter, arguably the most significant culture and news driver of our times in terms of impact, counting not only Presidents, but entire Governments, amongst its more than 317 million users.

Twitter's precursor, Odeo started as a company that would allow people to find and subscribe to podcasts. It was based on a technology, new at the time, that would enable a person to call a number and the recording of what was said (an early form of podcasting) would be posted on the Internet in MP3 format. Based on that one core product, Odeo was built as an entire podcasting platform solution. At the time, episodic audio content was proliferating, with the development of easy-to-access tools, but the content was difficult to find and aggregate. Even more, people wanting a convenient on-the-go method to access those recordings, mostly desired to have them in one place, and usually on their iPod, which at that time was still new to the market. The demand for iPod access eventually grew so much that what was previously known as "audioblogging" became inextricably connected to Apple with the terminology that we now use.

Many would likely be surprised to know that this currently ubiquitous term, "podcast" would only return 24 Google results if you did a search back on September 28, 2004. In fact, back then, technology blogger Doc Searls presciently stated on his blog, "But now most of my radio listening is to what Adam Curry and others are starting to call podcasts. That last link currently brings up 24 results on Google. A year from now, it will pull up hundreds of thousands, or perhaps even millions."[42] The development of the term "podcast" went way beyond Searls' predictions. A current Google search, as of this time of writing yields 296 million results.

What had initially appeared to be an incredible opportunity and common problem to solve for the Odeo team, became the seed of its demise. In June 2005, amidst the rapidly evolving technology landscape, Apple decided to disintermediate the aggregators, and launch its own podcasting platform on iTunes, which served to decimate the playing field for other players.[43] Circumstances had suddenly changed, and Odeo, overnight, had become irrelevant.

At the time, Odeo had already received funding from outside investors who were looking for a return on the money that they had put into the company. Confronted with a substantial circumstantial setback that was certain to end their original plan, rather than throw in the towel, with the money left in the bank, the Odeo team decided to tinker to find a new idea. This was the essence of their pivot. Odeo was going to be a goner, but in spite of dirty bathwater, they still had a baby, and that baby had legs. The core idea of mobile-to-podcast was used to spark several other ideas, including a project internally referred to as Twttr. It was conceived of by a then-staffer, Jack Dorsey, who became obsessed with the idea of the "status" announcement to friends – that concept of broadcasting "what am I doing now," "how am I feeling now," and "what am I thinking now" was the seed of the idea for Twitter.

Running low on cash and facing demanding investors, the team was far from out of the woods. At the time, early Twitter seemed like a meaningless idea, too far of a stretch for the imaginations of the board of directors, and was not developed enough of an asset for potential acquirers of Odeo. And here's where the story becomes even more interesting. When the board of directors failed to grasp the potential of Twitter, Evan Williams seized the opportunity. He sent a letter to the Odeo investors offering to make them whole in their investments, repurchasing the entire company equity, which he would now own 100% going forward. Using his personal capital to return an initial investment of $5 million, as well as to bankroll the fledgling company's first year of operations was a big risk. A few months later, Williams re-approached the original Odeo investors with an offer to participate in the funding of the new company at a new valuation of $25 million, a 5x increase over what Williams himself had paid.[44] Today, the company is worth over 2400 times the original investment.

This example of a pivot is helpful when thinking about facing different types of setbacks that are common in any endeavor. It is a wonderful way to quit what isn't working, but not give up on what is—to use what you have as a seed to develop into another branch along the path to success. Using the story as a reference, the pivot is comprised of the following elements:

- Identification of a key idea that is still interesting and worth pursuing
- Creation of options
- Identification of the "best bet"
- Commitment to move forward on the "best bet"

Notice that, as in the case of Evan Williams' decision to repurchase the equity of Odeo, even as it was failing, the pivot does require preparation in terms of having access to resources. In this case, Evan Williams had previously sold his prior company, Blogger, to Google for an undisclosed amount, which we can safely assume was in the millions. Not having access to millions of dollars, should be no excuse for anyone, however, as you've seen in the story of Sara Blakely, and will also see in a later story of another pivot that has created one of the best cafés in Paris. Just like we talked about in the Contingency Plan section in chapter 2, savings are important. It is going to be the fuel that you use to power the "best bet" amongst the options that you create. Making the sacrifices and finding the discipline to save are not easy, especially when income might be limited and necessary expenses can be unrelenting. But, you owe it to yourself to find a way. Think of it as purchasing your freedom – your freedom of choice, your freedom of a successful future and your freedom from lingering in failure.

In our next story, I want to show for those of us with fewer commas to count than Evan Williams, that savings can literally "save" you and send you on your way to success past seemingly impossible circumstances.

I met my good friend Jeff Marois during my time running a company called Atom Digital, which was a division of the management company for a number of very successful music artists, the most notable of which was Lady Gaga. At that time, my role was somewhat of a hybrid, requiring me to lead strategic digital projects for the management company's artists and other outside clients and companies, but also vet and evaluate the various technology startups that wanted to leverage the power of Lady Gaga's tens of millions of social media followers.

The company that Jeff had started was called Fanzy and it leveraged Facebook to allow fans of artists to earn social media credibility and status for their enthusiastic support of the artists that they loved.[45] I thought that the product was genius and ultimately a number of the management company's artists became clients. As for Jeff and I, we became friends and managed to stay in contact over the years.

As you can never control the circumstances, just as Jeff's product was starting to gain traction, similar to the events at Odeo, Facebook decided to make changes that disintermediated Fanzy and rendered the product ineffective. "I felt like the product wasn't strong enough and the timing was horrendous," Jeff said of his thoughts at the time.[46] "But, it wasn't just us [affected by the Facebook changes]; it was happening to everyone else also. If everyone else were doing great, and we were the only ones failing, then I would have thought of us more critically." Even after that point, for another year, Jeff and his team continued their work to look for an alternative use for the technology that had been developed. Unfortunately, the landscape was not amenable to any of the changes that they would have been able to make, especially given the amount of runway that was left in their bank account.

Although that year was the most challenging of all, Jeff was motivated to end well and maintain good relationships with his investors and employees. Eventually, Fanzy was dissolved. And while the story of the company concludes, the story of Jeff's success as an entrepreneur is just beginning.

Naturally curious and a businessman by nature and education, all throughout the process of building Fanzy, Jeff never stopped learning. He used his savings to make strategic investments, in smaller sums and occasionally in time, rather than money, in enterprises that presented him with the opportunity to learn about a new industry. As an example, he made a minority investment in a fledgling restaurant in his hometown of Paris, which eventually became a very popular and critically acclaimed seafood establishment. He made the investment because he wanted to know more about the food, hospitality, and restaurant business. Being an investor provided him with the opportunity to learn. Later, when a family member bought and refurbished a landmark Parisian hotel, Jeff contributed his time and assistance, which allowed him invaluable insight into that process as well.

With these investments of both money and time, when Fanzy entered challenging circumstances, much of the groundwork had already been inadvertently laid for the options that Jeff would later choose to pursue. But, first, he took a pause. "Although I spent time reconnecting, I mainly focused on doing nothing," he said. "The end of Fanzy was stressful. It was a lot of uncertainty and asking for money – and people saying no. It gets you down. When it ended, I took time for myself and explored options as an entrepreneur." Leading a startup, through the initial stages of proof of concept, and even the later phases of unending rounds of fundraising, business development, and troubleshooting can be exhausting. Leading a startup through a wind-down, through the emotionally-draining and devastating process of staff layoffs and dissolution can be extinguishing. He needed to give himself a break. So, he took some time for a focused recharge, pursuing his hobby of kitesurfing and travelling around to visit with friends. Alongside his relaxation and personal rehabilitation, Jeff continued to nurture his side project investments. By this time, the restaurant had proven quite successful and had provided a lucrative return. And the hotel business had highlighted a potential avenue to pursue.

Coupling his educational training at INSEAD, one of the world's top business and management graduate programs, alongside his professional experience having held roles as both an employee of a company and at the helm of his own startup, he felt confident that his next role would again be one that he created for himself. Throughout Paris and even in the midst of his kite surfing adventures in Lisbon, Jeff looked for his next investment opportunity, leveraging his network, talking to other entrepreneurs and friends, and exchanging ideas. Having taken the time to synthesize and internalize the lessons of his prior endeavor, he decided to focus efforts on starting a business for which he wouldn't have to regularly raise money, that would be profitable quickly without a long development lead-time, and could be established in an industry that evidenced a stable, obvious business model, that almost could run itself.

As he learned from working on a family project, a hotel could fit those characteristics. So, for almost two years, he searched for a hotel to purchase in either Paris or Lisbon—it was a careful balance to find the exactly right opportunity, a combination of good location and right price. But the perfect property never materialized. What did materialize was the opportunity to consult for other companies along the way, introducing him to new businesses and eventually, to his next investment, a fledgling coffee roaster in Paris, Belleville Brûlerie.

As an investor and advisor, Jeff helped his partners refine their business model, for top notch, great coffee (only the top 1% of the global production of coffee beans make the cut) with a conscious approach to their entire supply chain. Ironically, while the hotel idea didn't work in a way that would perfectly fit the characteristics that he had identified for his next venture, the coffee roasting business, at first just an investment, did fit exactly.

The business grew quickly, evolving into a hybrid roaster and café that the company purchased and opened, La Fontaine de Belleville, located in Paris' 10ème arrondissement (district). Both the roastery and the café have become a smashing success. The café has distinguished itself for its unique and hyper-local approach to the food and menu options that it provides as well as its heavy emphasis on service. They are currently evaluating options for a second location and have been nominated by *Sprudge. com* (the coffee-lovers community) as one of the best new cafés in the world for 2016.[47]

Jeff's pivot is a great example of what it means to Regroup in the face of changing circumstances and a path that is no longer working. Although he invested himself completely in building his first startup, Fanzy, it was by no means the only way to reach his goal of building and running a successful business. When the tide of technology turned against his product, he had the benefit of options that he had been cultivating all along, just by engaging his natural curiosity.

For some, this cultivation of options contradicts the common belief that if you create a Plan B, that you're not really committed to Plan A. This isn't necessarily true. Plan A is the current plan to reach Goal A, but *Plan A is not Goal A.* Learn to separate your goal from your plan. This will help you gain perspective, free up your creative energy and afford yourself the benefit of options so that you can quickly Regroup and find the next best path forward when you reach an obstacle or setback in the road. Pivoting is not in any way giving up. It is when you reach a conclusion on a *method* that is not working and find a better way to reach the same goal.

Persistence Vs. Stubbornness

There was once a man, Charles, who held closely to his religious faith. He believed in God and had a very clear view of how God would move and act in his life. One day, in the small town he lived in, local news began reports of a big and significant storm headed their way, threatening torrential rains and heavy flooding. All residents were advised to evacuate immediately. Charles, rooted in his beliefs, watched the reports but said to himself, "I'm going to stay put. God will save me."

Later that evening, his neighbor knocked on the door and said, "I heard there was a big storm approaching, wanna ride with me? I'm getting out of here."

Charles replied, "Thank you, but I'm staying put. God is going to save me." Early the next morning, the storm began. Water fell from the sky in sheets, and sure enough, began to collect and cover the roads with massive puddles. When he heard a knock on the door, he rushed to answer it. In front of him stood an officer from the local police department with a warning to leave for higher ground. Charles thanked the officer, but sent him away, thinking to himself, *I'm not going anywhere, God will save me.*

The waters began to rise as the storm only grew in strength. Charles had to move to the upper level of his house as the flood creeped into his home. A member of the local rescue team on a rowboat came by and knocked on a window. Holding tightly to his vision and faith in what would come to pass, Charles stayed put.

Eventually, the water level forced Charles to the roof of his home – the National Guard helicopter flew above, dropping down a rope. "TAKE THE ROPE!" They screamed to him desperately. But even then, Charles refused. He stayed put. And, ultimately, he drowned.

When he reached Heaven, Charles made it a point to seek God out. He had some serious questions that needed answering. "God, how was it that you let me drown? I stayed rooted in my faith, and waited for you to save me, but you never showed up."

In reply to Charles, God said, *"But my son, I sent you a neighbor, the police, a boat and a helicopter, what more would you have wanted me to do?"*

This story illustrates the danger of allowing stubbornness to prevent you from embracing flexibility. And you'll need flexibility to develop a new path towards your goal. Very seldom is true success a linear path. It is, instead, a sporadic course. When our minds become fixated on a certain ideal rather than being flexible enough to evaluate outcomes and explore the opportunities in difficult moments, we run the risk of closing off our saving grace.

Persistence means gradually chipping away at the objective through twists and turns; but stubbornness means staying on the same path because you're too proud, too reluctant or too fearful to take a step forward into the unknown. It's the very definition of insanity: doing the *same* thing and expecting a different result. You have to do a *different* thing to get a different result. Consider Thomas Edison's perspective on invention, "I haven't failed; I've only found 10,000 ways that wouldn't work." These were 10,000 different ways – not the same way 10,000 times. Persistence is a partner to perspective, but stubbornness makes you blind.

So, how do you determine whether a pivot makes sense for you? Consider the following questions:

> For this attempt, is there still an active goal in your mind? Are there questions that remain unanswered? Things you still haven't tried?
>
> Does your passion remain or could you easily recapture it after a bit of recuperation?
>
> Do you have, or could you create additional options that might fit a larger vision for your life?
>
> Did this attempt bring you even a *little* bit closer to your larger goal?

If at least some of these answers are yes, you likely have enough of the spark left over to power you into a new direction. Pivoting means that you know deep down, in some way or another that you don't want to quit, and this decision ensures that you don't have to.

But, what about situations in which most of your answers to the questions above are negative? It doesn't mean that you need to give up. But, it may mean that you need a different kind of option, one that gives you a break in a way that frees you up to pursue something else. It's not giving up, but it is giving yourself an out.

The Quit

The word "quit" is something that we shun and turn away from in contemporary society. Its connotation is one of loss, of defeat, and of being overwhelmed by circumstances that could not be surmounted. It is the very foundation of being a Failure: a quitter. We are nearly all familiar with the adage: "Quitters never win." Well, in the concept of a Regroup, there is room for quitting as well, just not how we typically think about it.

We generally only want to quit when things are going badly. Very few people, other than those with superhuman discipline at the tables in Vegas, have any desire to quit while they are ahead. Instead, the desire to quit comes at a moment of loss, of setback coupled with overwhelming negative and painful emotions.

Some of that pain and negative emotion is caused by the sting of losing, and some by the cascade of negative thinking that we explored earlier. The desire to quit is the mind's reaction to negativity, looking for the quickest end to the pain and discomfort. The desire to quit, boiled down, is a reactionary force seeking to direct us back to the comfort that we knew before we stumbled.

There is nothing wrong with wanting to quit—it is a natural reaction to a negative circumstance. Where you stand to lose is not *choosing* how and when you quit. To quit in *direct* response to negative emotion is the very essence of giving up. It is allowing your negative feelings to push you towards comfort, giving in to your mind's assessment that you are in danger by pursuing goals that are still out of reach. It is the core illusion that is introduced by a setback.

Affording yourself the ability to choose how, when and if you quit is the very essence of what a Regroup is—to enter a space where you never have to give up, even if you do decide, on *your own terms* and in *your own timing*, to quit. It is a space free from the pressure of negative emotions. You absolutely can quit and not give up, so long as you quit truly by *choice*.

The reality is, sometimes a setback comes when all of the lessons have been learned, when all of the pressing questions have been answered and when all of the truly inspirational experiences of a particular endeavor have been extinguished. It can come when you've had a taste of something that you thought would be great, that you believed would deliver you to a certain place, but, after really getting to know the circumstances, you learned better. Where you know you could find a better way, and that you *will* find a better way. A controlled quit doesn't mean that you're giving up on your goal; it just means that you've found one of the 10,000 ways that haven't worked.

The *never quit on your worst day* rule is a great standard to follow because it recognizes the reality that quitting may be a practical solution, but also emphasizes that it must be you, not your subconscious mind and not your emotions that makes the decision.

This process was beautifully illustrated in Hampus Jakobsson's post which I referenced previously. As he described the process of how his company folded, I was struck by how thoughtful and intentional he and his team were. It was important for him to end well, making sure in the process they followed, that everyone would receive the maximum benefit of all of the lessons learned and experience gained. Knowing that the team was exhausted and the passion was lost, their path forward was not the one they originally intended or wanted to follow, but it was honored by a thoughtful strategy.

In many of my own endeavors, I can't say I've been as graceful. Learning how not to quit on my worst day has been the cornerstone of my success as an entrepreneur. It has also been central to my development as a person. Most of the things that I quit, especially when I was younger, I regret, like piano lessons, singing in the choir, trying to master guitar, and my first blog. But sometimes, the smartest thing is to give up what you don't need, to focus on what you do.

I have a friend who was miserable at her job. Her boss was a menace and she felt as though her contributions were overlooked when it came time for promotions and raises. She was ready to quit. But, conventional workplace wisdom says you don't quit one job until you have another. And so, she stayed, all the while polishing up her resume and interviewing for other positions. During that time, her boss wound up leaving for another employer, and she eventually got her promotion.

As it turns out, the process of interviewing for other jobs increased her confidence in her own abilities. The current position no longer seemed like such a burden and felt more like an option, with upside and downside. But she had created other options for herself as well, and could weigh them all alongside one another.

Taking the option not to quit on your worst day affords you the opportunity to net out all of the lessons in your experience and to stay in position long enough to allow chance to swing in your favor. You never know what changed circumstances the next day will bring. Imagine what could happen if you allow yourself to see it? Quitting on controlled terms is another form of Regrouping that allows you to manage changed circumstances while keeping your larger goal or dream intact. It allows you to let go of what isn't working to focus more clearly on what is. It is important to honor and allow your negative emotions; they are telling you that something is not right about the path you're pursuing. It's also as important *not to be controlled* by them.

How to Quit

Quitting can be a process, a rewarding one, if you approach it that way. In order to do that, at the time of a setback, given the strong negative emotions and thoughts that swirl, if you feel like you want to quit, the first thing to do is allow that feeling and entertain the thought. Don't act on the impulse, but engage in the purely mental exercise. Assume that you were going to act on how you feel. In this particular circumstance, what would it mean to quit? Does it mean affirmatively doing something? Does it mean not doing something? Does it mean not fulfilling an existing obligation? Is the next immediate step to take something that you absolutely cannot do, or is it something that you simply do not *want* to do?

As I have found in my own experience, in the times that I most wanted to quit, the next step was not something that I could not do – in fact, the next step was fairly minor. The problem was that I did not want to do it. I was uncomfortable and wanted the discomfort to end immediately. If you've reached a place that the next step is something you cannot do, you've reached a stopping point that you didn't create. If you cannot continue, then this point might be the best time for you to gather yourself, process your lessons and use that information to develop an approach to your next attempt. If you can continue, then not quitting is simply the force of will to take the next logical step, because you can.

Operating the force of will gives you options. You have the

option to continue, and you have the option to quit. Either way, you have the ability to ensure that the option you pick will best serve your interests, objectives and goals, while maintaining your integrity.

To develop quitting as an option, you'll need to evolve a "quitting plan" for yourself. This sets up your terms for quitting, your where, when and how to protect your interests, and your integrity. It allows you to honor your feelings and carefully evaluate your desire to quit. But, in the same token, it prevents your feelings from controlling you.

The first step in your quitting plan is to select the date on which you'll quit. If the process of developing continuing as an option doesn't create benefits that outweigh quitting, then pick a day to make the final call. I suggest giving yourself at least thirty days. That amount of time affords a long enough window to give random and possible favorable surprises a chance to happen that could change your circumstances. Aside from allowing chance to swing in your favor, you want to capture the full benefit of any personal growth and learning during this time.

Reaching the point that you want to quit is tantamount to reaching the point where your muscles start to ache in the gym. You haven't yet reached the point of muscle failure, where you actually couldn't physically manage to lift the weight again even with all of your effort. You're simply at the place where the pain is starting to build and the discomfort has made itself known as a pressing concern. As most trainers will tell you, this is actually the point of transformation. That discomfort is the signal that you've reached the threshold of the narrow range of opportunity. This is the time to make the most of your experience, to push as far as you can toward transformation to see the results of your work. As long as you can stand it, try to stay there to extract the benefit of the lessons that you have *earned*.

No matter how long you decide, once you have your date, you can return to developing the further details of quitting beyond the obvious, like your how and what next steps you'll need to consider in continuing toward your goal. Once you have made the decision to quit, and to quit responsibly, there's nothing more for you to worry about. Shift your energy to what's ahead of you rather than what you've placed in your rear-view mirror.

Lose the Battle to Win the War

Never giving up is a combination of purpose, mindset, passion, and resources. The latter ingredient, resources, might be infinite over time; but, for most people, the opposite is true in the immediate, and especially when facing a setback. As we've previously explored, setbacks erode our confidence and set off a chain reaction in our minds that trigger our self-protection mechanisms. At that point, not giving up becomes its own war – not just against circumstances, but against the narrative composed by your own mind. Fighting that war, for your vision and the realization of your dreams and objectives takes many resources of time, energy, and expertise. To say the least, it's exhausting. If you know that a certain path is not working, ending that road deliberately saves your remaining resources to fight another day. As we've learned from history, most of the great wars that were fought and ultimately lost after many battles, result from a dwindling of resources, rather than other factors.

Success is simply exercising the will and the perseverance required to reach a worthwhile end objective. Failure is the point at which you give up.

Inherent in the concept of the lean approach to startups is the encouragement to fail quickly. The unspoken element of that advice, after you've failed quickly, is: ...and try something else.

Chapter 7:
Map Out Your Next Move

When I left my position at the digital strategy and marketing agency that I had built over the preceding 12 months, it was in the final stages of executive producing a very successful project that had been initiated for Lady Gaga. That project ultimately won 10 prestigious marketing awards, including a Webby, three Davey Awards, three W3 Awards and an OMMA. It was *Gaga's Workshop* for Barneys New York. While not my choice of timing, I had to make the decision that was best for me and that most honored who I wanted to be and what I felt that I was worth. With the sudden departure, I hadn't really had time to map out my next move or even think about where I wanted to go from where I left off. All I knew was that I wanted to leverage my own skills for myself and that I wanted to create the best that I could in the world, whatever I did next.

Ultimately, I decided to build upon my experience by launching my own agency that would focus on clients I found exciting. I set my standards for the companies with which I would work and on which I would focus my attention. It was a combination of a pivot and a goal change. And although it happened over a consolidated period of time, my next steps incorporated a working understanding of lessons learned following my own short debriefing on how everything had come to pass.

My first step was to set up my options and critically assess the resources that would be needed for each potential option.

Mapping out your next move is essentially a planning process that incorporates the lessons you've learned to illuminate the next best steps forward. You're going to need to take inventory of what is available to you, as well as what you need in order to line up your resources for the next push. This next step also presents opportunities to evidence your growth and your willingness to expand beyond your limitations and fears.

What's Your Next Best Step?

As we saw in the example of Jeff in a previous chapter, as well as my own example in the section above, the most valuable takeaway of any challenging experience is a clear understanding of what to do differently the next time. This should be what comes of your own debrief. Jeff, for example, knew exactly what kind of business model he wanted to pursue and that led him to his current business, which fits the framework he outlined. In my own example, I managed to narrow down what was most important to me in moving forward, that in addition to building my own brand with my next venture, I also wanted to maximize the good that I did. This is what led me to write my previous book, *Piece of the Fame*. My goal was to synthesize the most critical lessons for social media and brand building into a resource that anyone could use. That book led to opportunities including traveling around the world, new business engagements and ultimately, the incredible experience of re-building the Cosmedicine brand.

To help determine your next best step, consider the following questions:

Based on your key takeaways from your experience, what are the top three things that you would do differently?

What improvement in result would you expect from implementing those changes?

What new resources do you need to move forward?

Set up Your Options

Once you know what direction you're going to take, this is the time to start assembling your resources behind the best available options. If you haven't been creating options all along, this is the time to start. I would recommend developing at least two possibilities at the same time, provided that you can manage the demands of both competently.

Manage Your Resources

<u>Money</u>

Most would say that money is the most significant resource they need. Money is the assurance that the gap between what you need or want and what you have will be filled. I must stress the necessity of creating a pool of savings as a seed to ensure that you're able to carry on as needed. Not only do you need emergency savings as a backstop for your living necessities, but you also need savings to pursue options for your advancement.

Nothing is more frustrating than to have a great idea that you'd like to move forward with, or to have dreamt up the perfect solution to a problem that you've faced in the past, and then realize you have no means to carry through. Think of that feeling of frustration every time you come in front of something that you want to purchase. And make a decision about that investment. It's hard to delay gratification, especially in advance of needing the savings. It's a tough world out there and we all deserve an occasional treat as a reward for hard work and sacrifice. And for many, simply making ends meet doesn't leave any left over for savings. Find a way, even if it boils down to a piggy bank. Whether you buy simple necessities or stock, make the investment in yourself first and always.

Time

Time is the only resource that is truly scarce. You can conserve it, and save it, but you can't increase it. This means that sacrifices must be considered and made to move forward on your options. It may come down to difficult choices such as time with friends or family, or even time for yourself. It's a selfish choice that you have to decide is important enough to make. Your natural limitations on time might play a central role in what options you elect to develop and pursue. That's still fine. Even with every single possible constraint that you could have, there's still an option for you. You just have to find it.

Expertise

Is there something that you need to learn or an unanswered question that would otherwise inform your direction? Fortunately, we live in an information age where the answers to your greatest questions are at best a few keystrokes away, and no worse than a trip to your local library. Just recently I read an article about a woman with no prior experience, who built a five-bedroom, 3500 square foot home by watching YouTube videos.[48] Seriously. There are so many resources for free education. If you are not availing yourself of them, you are missing out on one of the *greatest* and best developments of our time. Anyone can learn almost anything, just by finding the right resources online. And arguably, they must engage in this learning just to keep pace with the rapid technological advancements of today's society. The *New York Times* quoted AT&T Chairman Randall Stephenson as saying, "There is a need to retool yourself, and you should not expect to stop." He also noted that if you don't dedicate at least five to ten hours each week to learning online, you will be amongst the people who "will obsolete themselves with the technology."[49] Because the world is changing at such a rapid clip, we are all being forced to adopt learning as a lifestyle, rather than just a phase that we go through in our youth.

I remember having a conversation with a friend who, while telling me about her startup, told me that also, at over 40 years old and as a former entertainment executive, she literally taught herself how to code. She didn't learn this new skill to get a new job – it was to build her own digital platform that was required to move forward with her own company. This is something that you can do as well. Anybody can. Resources are everywhere.

If rapper Prince Harvey could record his entire album using the display computers at an Apple store in New York City after his computer died (twice) and his hard drive was stolen, you too can make a way out of no way.[50]

Energy

The energy that you'll need for your plan going forward is of two kinds – physical and mental. The concept of physical energy is fairly straightforward. It's the physical endurance and stamina required to possibly do double and triple duty as you work on your options.

The second kind of energy that you'll need, the mental energy, is based on how you feel on the inside, rather than how you physically feel. However, each can affect and be affected by the other. In order to maximize your mental and emotional energy, you'll need to focus on the positive, whether it's your goal and related affirmations, or enlightening and inspiring music, books and other content. It's what you'll use to lift your mood and your spirits.

To focus on the positive, it is also as important to minimize the negative. That means minimizing your exposure to forceful discouragers, and lining up your forceful congratulators. After you've done all the work of previous chapters in managing your mind, you don't want to have to battle negative external sources of doubt, discouragement and judgment. The weight of that negativity, especially multiplied by the propensity of your mind is enough to derail even the most well-crafted plan. So do yourself a favor, and protect the fragile hope and light that you are able to generate for yourself and focus your attention on only that which magnifies it.

Relationships

Take inventory of your relationships. Who can you call on? In my previous book, *Piece of the Fame*, I discussed segmentation of your contacts into: "who knows you," "who likes you," and "who loves you." In the process of your Regroup, this is your opportunity to find out who those people are and give them the opportunity to help you.

<u>Ask</u>

In April 2012, after a period of building a substantial online audience, Amanda Palmer exploded in fame, having raised nearly $1.2 Million via crowdfunding platform Kickstarter to pay for the costs of her upcoming album. This mindboggling result evolved into a *TED* talk and then later, a *New York Times* best-selling book, *The Art of Asking*. In her time as a very well-known public figure, she has not escaped more than her fair share of controversy, and, perhaps, even courted it. What has not been controversial, however, has been her sometimes radical message promoting vulnerability and actually asking friends, associates, colleagues and acquaintances for help.

The fine line between asking and begging has always been razor thin. While asking seems to be acceptable, begging seems to come with some sort of shame attached to it – as if there's a threshold crossed by the combination of asking and actually needing what was asked for. Those that would otherwise ask, do not for fear of somehow inadvertently treading over into the territory of begging, or becoming a charity case. And it may be true that in our society, we think of our charity as reserved for those who are significantly less fortunate than us. But if we accept this absolutely, then what about our brother or sister, or friend or Facebook friend, for that matter who also needs help, but perhaps not our "charity?" Perhaps even if someone extended an offer to help *you*, pride would require you to refuse, for fear of becoming someone's *charity case.*

This is something that we all need to mend and heal from as a collective community. We have embraced these extremes relating to giving and asking for help that do not serve us or bring us closer together. It creates a wedge and illusion of the necessity of complete self-reliance that drives us further apart. Asking for what you need does not automatically make you a charity case, especially when you're asking someone who already knows you.

Consider, your close friend whom you care about asks you to help him move. It's a Saturday and it's raining. You've worked 70 hours the week prior and are exhausted, but you do it anyway. Why? Do you view your actions as charity? Perhaps your friend feels bad about asking you, but he doesn't have other options, so he really had no choice. Do you view him as a charity case? Why or why not? Allowing yourself to reexamine your presumptions about asking for help may aid in making progress toward eliminating the fear of reaching out to others with a request.

Early on, I made the decision to launch this book through a crowdfunding effort. It wasn't about specifically needing the budget, it was about needing and soliciting the support from the people that I knew or was connected to. I was terrified. I have nearly 2000 Facebook friends, some close connections, some work associates, some were people that I had connected to but didn't have a strong relationship with. What I did not realize prior to starting the campaign was that regardless of whether I knew my contact well or not, and regardless of whether I could count on that person to be there for me in a time of need, for some reason I cared what they thought. And this concern, this fear of judgment that I was somehow a charity case for soliciting their purchases and pledges was irrational.

Like Who Likes You. Love Who Loves You

The process of crowdfunding forced me to do the one thing that I had avoided for years. I was always the first one to offer help to others – to support, to cheer on, to buy one (or two), to share and spread the word, but when it came to asking others when I needed something, I often was hesitant to even send an email announcement. I thought that I was bothering them, or that they would get angry, or decide for the intrusion that they no longer desired to have that connection with me. This phobia – an irrational fear of something that actually doesn't present a threat, was not something I wanted to continue. And since I could identify it, I decided that I would chase it down, and demand a confrontation.

The campaign forced me to email directly and individually

nearly all 2000 people that I have even the most remote connection to. In addition to emailing, for those whose numbers I
had, I called, sent texts and follow up messages. The calls went
out and the pledges to my campaign came back. In many cases,
people who I didn't even think of as close, pledged hundreds of
dollars just to help birth my then-nascent idea for a little book
that would teach people how to Regroup. Within 10 days, I had
52 backers, with pledges ranging from $5 to $500 and everything
in-between. The biggest reward, however, was not the money. It
was the conversations that I had with people that I hadn't spoken
to in a while. When you call to ask for something, it forces you
to take the time and really talk – to open yourself, to create an
doorway into your life and your thoughts – to stretch your own
comfort zone.

Notwithstanding having raised over $5,000, the campaign
failed to reach the goal. It was disappointing and at first, a little
embarrassing. If nothing else, there was clearly something that I
didn't know about how to run a successful *Kickstarter* campaign
for a book project. But, I also knew that there was *no way* I would
let a failed *Kickstarter* campaign stop me from completing an important goal. As you have already realized, since you are reading
the book that the failed campaign was intended to fund, I moved
forward anyway. I made some adjustments and found another
way to make it work. Although the crowdfunding effort failed, I
had learned valuable information about best practices for the future. Most important, I discovered that some people that I hadn't

spoken to in years supported me more than I ever knew and it was time to allocate more resources to investing in my *existing* relationships.

Asking for help does more than get you help; it provides the only opportunity available to do the work of releasing some of the fears that we hold toward each other. It is a small experiment that you can conduct to learn how to successfully navigate this space with others. It connects; and yes, it exposes. Make no mistake, asking is an experiment; no matter how well you think you know the person that you're asking, you still run the risk of being turned down. It's their choice, and they don't owe you anything. If you think of asking for help as extending an opportunity to that person to say yes, you can better manage the expectations about what you'll receive on the other end. What I hope for you is that you find something in your life that means so much to you and that is so worthwhile that it forces you to ask for help because it is too big and too great for you to do on your own – and even better, for you to want to do on your own.

Chapter 8:
Commit to Continue

*None of my inventions came by accident. I see a worthwhile
need to be met and I make trial after trial until it comes.'
What it boils down to is one per cent inspiration and nine-
ty-nine per cent perspiration.*[51]

– Thomas Edison

I n the process of doing anything great, uncertainty always
precedes advancement. It is the experience of finding a
new way. This can be exciting and at the same time, in-
timidating due to the challenges and setbacks of unanticipated
outcomes. This is when the idea of "impossible" seems most likely
to be true. As we Regroup, we learn that belief in the impossible
is as much of a faith as the belief that everything is possible. And

the latter leaves room for necessary hope and optimism.

The mind is entrusted with ensuring our survival, and as a vestige of our hunter-gatherer natures, it consistently pressures us to conserve resources. This tendency toward conservation of resources drives us to make unnecessary trade-offs and draw premature conclusions. The resources that truly power success have never been scarce: passion, hope, faith, intelligence, and the time to try one more thing.

Through all of its examples, anecdotes and instruction, this book has really only been about one thing – the mastery of mind and the navigation of negative emotions that can weigh heavily enough to break our resolve. It is a tool set, a resource to keep you on course. When you believe you can't, this book's aim is to help you find one possible way to say and believe that you can. And with that spark, you can light the fire that is a commitment to continue.

With each step forward in the face of adversity, you strengthen your internal pledge that no matter what, you will not now, not ever, give up. And you'll do this, knowing that rather than pursuing a fool's errand, your emotions and the lessons along the way will help to keep you on a productive path. It's a self-directed form of trust that can be built each time you regain your footing following a stumble. Eventually, you learn that you may fall, but you certainly will stand up again and keep marching. Even if you decide to pause and rest, pivot in a new direction, or quit and try again from a different starting place, you hold on to your purpose and stay committed to your dream. As famed writer Oliver Goldsmith is credited with saying, "Success consists of getting up just one more time than you fall."

Redefining Your What and Reconnecting with Your Why

In making the commitment to continue you have the opportunity to reexamine the key questions that will provide the fuel that you need to keep going.

What fundamental problem are you trying to solve?

Who does solving the problem help?

What does helping those people mean to you?

No matter your answers to the questions above, the strongest commitments always boil down to a why that connects to people. If you haven't gotten there, then your problem may not be big enough *yet*. It will be up to you to expand your perspective and broaden your solution so that the pull to be of service awakens your soul and enlists its cooperation.

This step is your engine. Once you've mapped out your path, this will be the power plant that will electrify your journey through to the next place.

Back at my last semblance of a traditional corporate job, albeit at a record company, my coworkers and I created a gigantic lottery pool whenever the jackpot surged over $300 Million. We would all gather our money and someone would rush to the local convenience store to purchase an accordion of tickets. We'd each get a photocopy of our entries and would eagerly await the results. For us at that time, those photocopies were more than just numbers, they were dreams—of vacations, of private school tuition, of new homes and better accommodations for aging parents. They were freedom. We thought that in the lottery, we could find our chance to be free from what we saw as the monotonous "shackles" of a nine-to-five, and instead be liberated from the regret of looking out of the window at a life seemingly better lived. We thought that $300 Million (split 10 ways) would be the sizable sum we needed to buy our way out of the most expensive curse known to wo/man – regret.

As it turns out, in spite of the many tickets that were purchased, and the many wishes put upon those numbers, we never won. Despite this, another one of my colleagues and I would not be deterred. We wanted an escape and we wanted it badly. She wanted a different environment and the opportunity to fulfill some of her life dreams. I wanted one thing and one thing only, the freedom of my time and geography. The one and only purchase that I would make with my lottery winnings was to buy back my time. To me, this was the most valuable. At this time, the book *The Secret* had come to market and it was all about the power of positive thinking and visualization. So I visualized and visualized and visualized. And, instead of saving each of those dollars that I could, I spent them on lottery tickets, $5 a week.

While we would continue to play the lottery regularly, I started to progress a little further with my visualization practice, and began a purposeful course of prayer and intention setting. Looking for more information and insight, I came across a very interesting book, *Write it Down, Make it Happen* by Henriette Klauser. So, I started writing it down, day after day, in a spiral notebook: *God, please grant me the freedom of my time and geography*. And then, right under that, I would write the very same thing again: *God, please grant me the freedom of my time and geography*. And then I'd do it again, and again, and again, until an entire notebook had been filled with what would have definitely looked to an outsider like the scribbling of a madwoman. I'm sure during that time, people would have walked by my office and seen me hard at work on my desk writing something very long and very intense, by hand – little did they know that it was me writing my own escape plans.

For over a year, I wrote and wrote – as my *why* had become very clear, "freedom of my time and geography," it was easy for me to articulate it and repeat it to God, myself and to anyone else that would listen. Now, I happen to be Christian, born and raised. So to me, a natural relationship with the God that I know is second nature. I speak to Him and he shows up in force in my life. It's my belief and it has worked for me. For you, I would never want you to think that this is the *only way* to effectuate the honing of your desires. What I call prayer, we in our society and in other religions, call many other things: meditation, affirmations, mantras and more. These formed thoughts and clearest desires can be spoken, written, repeated in our minds, or sung, according to the many methods of focusing them into your own being. For me, I got crystal clear with a laser focus on what I wanted. I wrote my prayer and I wrote it to *God*.

All during that time of writing, we continued to play the lottery, even up until my last day of work, when I had been moved to quit and launch myself out of a life of dissatisfied comfort, into my next dance in the realm of uncertainty. I never won the lottery. Yet, since 2011, I have worked from wherever I wanted in the world with complete autonomy over how I spend each and every one of my days. I can't say that I haven't done anything I didn't want to do, or spent time anywhere I didn't want to be. I did. There were many days that I had to do things that I didn't particularly feel like doing or like very much; but, they were necessary to the project I was working on, and the project was directly related to my goal. For this reason, I was able to accomplish them with joy. On the sporadic days when I found myself in places that I would prefer not to visit – it was never longer than a day or two and most certainly at the airport once I left, I always had my choice of destination. I always chose forward towards the realization of my purpose.

I didn't get to take the express chute to my goal, but I still got there right on time. How I lost the lottery but still won the jackpot is detailed not only in this chapter, but in the story of the very many twists and turns that I've had to navigate along the way. It hasn't been about luck or huge wins; but instead, a regular pattern of taking risks, and figuring out my way past setbacks. That's how I stay afloat and keep myself on the path toward my dreams – not by winning the lottery, but by willing the pursuit of my why.

Be Relentless

Many of the great achievements in the world were accomplished by tired and discouraged men [and women] who kept on working.

– Unknown

Being relentless does not mean being tireless. Being relentless means mounting a resistance to resistance. Implicit in the word is the concept of self-care and along with it, having the ability to Regroup. As we've explored it, Regrouping does not always entail just powering through it. Sometimes it does mean taking a pause and sometimes it means changing the path entirely.

What many people call taking risks, I call *experiments*. How else will you learn if you don't try different avenues? Most people decide to focus on running only one experiment at a time, and it is usually bigger than they realize in terms of impact upon their life. We've been given a prescription of what we're *supposed* to do, without realizing that even this carries no guarantee.

When the perceived risk is low, people don't internalize the fact that there is a risk at all. They're running the experiment of working at their current job with the hopes that they'll advance, get a promotion and not be laid off unexpectedly with nothing to show for it. They're running the experiment of getting a particular kind of education with the expectation that the results will pay off enough to cover the debt that they incur. They're running the experiment of building a business around this one great idea with the hopes that it will be the one that works based on a current or conceivable plan. They're running the experiment of buying a house with the expectation that the market won't crash, that the value will rise and that no life changes will happen that will change their ability to meet the mortgage obligations. No matter how traditional the path, and however low the risk might be perceived to be, there is still *some* risk. Why not run an experiment of *your* choice at the same time?

My pattern of running riskier experiments has required me to learn to have several more than just one going at a time. This way, if I find out that one is not working, I have others in process, and the benefit of a new data point. No need in rerunning a failed experiment if we know that one way doesn't work. To make this approach productive, learning the lesson and making an adjustment for the next experiment lights the way to the next step forward. Being relentless involves sparing yourself the frustration of rerunning failed experiments—try something new. Move forward, don't stay in the same place. Use your time wisely by committing to never running just one experiment at the same time.

Nothing in this world can take the place of persistence. Talent will not; nothing is more common than unsuccessful people with talent. Genius will not; unrewarded genius is almost a proverb. Education will not; the world is full of educated derelicts. Persistence and determination alone are omnipotent. The slogan "press on" has solved and always will solve the problems of the human race.

– Calvin Coolidge

In May of 2014, Sophia Amoruso published the hardcover first edition of her book *#GIRLBOSS*. It was a smashing success and in it, she took a much deserved victory lap of 239 pages detailing the rise of her multimillion dollar company, Nasty Gal, a clothing retailer. By November 2016, that same company had filed for Chapter 11 Bankruptcy protection. Sophia, who from Nasty Gal's inception in 2006 until 2015 had been the CEO, was reported to be ceding her position as executive chairwoman appurtenant to the development. On the day of the announcement, she tweeted, "A decade above the influence. Onward babies. I love you."[52] At a conference the following day in Australia, she said:

"Things that I would have freaked out about two years ago I can handle now… Hopefully that is how I feel two years from now about this. It was my first business. I got really far."[53]

To understand the magnitude of this development, you should know of Nasty Gal that it was often used as an example of a stratospheric rise in growth and a symbol of what we would call "success." Even prior to her *New York Times* bestseller, Amoruso was named to *Forbes* "30 Under 30" list as well as its list of "Richest Self-Made Women." In 2012 Nasty Gal sales had grown an almost unbelievable nearly five-fold over the prior year to $100 Million. In 2015, revenue was reported by *Forbes* as exceeding $300 Million.[54] Over a period of three years, the company was credited with raising over $65 Million in venture capital investment. In spite of this success, missteps along the way turned into larger developments: bad workplace reviews on Glassdoor, lower than expected sales in brick and mortar retail locations, and ultimately the CEO swap-out for Sheree Waterson, all boded bad news for Nasty Gal. And while the writing was on the wall for the company, a different type of writing was beginning to emerge for Sophia.

She might not have been able to ultimately save Nasty Gal, but she had managed to begin a new experiment along the way—a new brand #GIRLBOSS. While still CEO of Nasty Gal, *#GIRLBOSS*, the book, was released in hardcover in 2014, followed by the paperback in 2015, followed by #Girlboss audio in 2015 as well. In 2016, Netflix announced that it would produce a series, to debut in 2017 based on the book, with Amoruso serving as executive producer. As one experiment was failing, a parallel experiment was starting to take off. She had created for herself her own pivot moment that would allow her options far beyond the reach of Nasty Gal's creditors. Options that would allow her to continue to pursue her passion and dreams. Wouldn't you call that a success?

> *Great entrepreneurs are like Indiana Jones. They take leaps*
> *before seeing the bridge because they know that if they don't,*
> *someone else will get that holy grail.*
>
> — Sophia Amoruso in #GIRLBOSS

Sophia Amoruso's tenacity at the end of Nasty Gal is the same grit and determination that could have been observed at the beginning. Although she had dropped out of school, been fired from multiple jobs, and made a minefield of mistakes (culminating in a dramatic end to her arguably first "career" as a shoplifter), each experience played its own role in the development of her vision for Nasty Gal, even the shoplifting. Her personal story is one of multiple failures and roadblocks, along with now multiple inarguable successes built upon her own vision and relentless execution.

> *"If at first you don't succeed, try and try again (just some-*
> *thing different this time)."*
>
> — Proverb, with my own modification

If at first you *do* succeed, try something different, just in case. Being relentless is built on determination, but it is fed by your overall *why* and a problem-solving approach to setbacks and obstacles. It comes from being laser-focused on the goal ahead and refusing to let any condition hold you back, pull you away or force you into submission. This never-say-die attitude will keep you in the game and make sure that odds are forever in your favor.

Beware of Comfort

As you seek the highest reaches of your purpose, keep diligent watch for the lulling comfort of *almost there*. This is what will threaten to derail you far beyond the worst moment of a setback. When your goal is in sight, just beyond the horizon, when you begin to feel the warming rays of its completion – this is the time to strengthen your resolve and press forward. Consider the story of Sophia Amoruso – had she grown comfortable in the success and growth of Nasty Gal, she would have never begun developing her options to press forward with the #GIRLBOSS brand.

Being almost there is so alluring. After suffering through a challenging climb, one might be tempted to relax and bask in the accomplishments of a job seemingly well done. But, as we have seen, the riches of the lessons, insights and perspectives to be gained happen at the point of discomfort. If you're not uncomfortable in some way, you're not growing. Don't let getting almost there stop you from actually getting all the way there. Keep chasing the horizon of your growth and you'll create a current of options that will ensure and maintain a continuous path forward.

There is something that I always say to the musicians and artists that I have had the profound pleasure of working with, *"go ahead and get your boos."* Often, especially at the start of their careers, artists are tentative about their stage performance – it elicits fear, concern and a cascade of "what ifs." It almost never fails to happen. Artists hone their craft for years, develop music and a fan base and people want to see them and experience them in person. When the art of the live performance is still a young muscle, it's quite stressful, as self-imposed anxieties build about how the audience will react, will the music or performance translate, and ultimately, most important, will their fans leave feeling the way they came to feel? What if expectations are not met?

Taking a page out of what I learned in my brief time in the world of standup comedy, I always say some version of the following:

Go ahead and take the stage. Don't worry because you are powerful. You have more power at that moment on stage than any one member in the audience. They all think that you are there to serve them, but the entire time, no matter what happens, you'll know the truth: that, in reality, they are there to serve you. Give the best that you can now and take from them what they came to give — their feedback. Gain experience and learn. Go and get your applause, or your boos. Either way, you are going to get something invaluable. They are going to give you the gift of their reaction to the experience you create. That's road under your tires on the way to stardom. You have the power to get better. You control when you get back into your room and practice, when you take your next voice lesson, practice your choreography and write your next best song. And as long as you commit to just one more time of taking the stage after this, you've already won.

Just like Beyoncé, in the aftermath of her loss on *Star Search*, never get comfortable in your failure or your success. Keep writing your own story and marching forward along your path to your dreams.

> *"The size of your success is measured by the strength of your desire, the size of your dream; and how you handle disappointment along the way."*
>
> – Robert Kiyosaki

People hear stories of success, but are often looking at the wrong data points and failing to ask the right questions to get the most benefit out of the story. By the time you intersect with most people's stories of success, you miss the point of how it could be relevant to you. We spend time detailing the accomplishments, instead of focusing on how that person made it past adversity, how they developed their attitude towards setbacks and failure and how they ultimately made progress. If it is not by attitude, then it is by process, and you need to find out what that process is. Their process now, but specifically their process when things were uncertain, when money was scarce, when accomplishments were few and far between, and when they were still navigating "no." Because once you get to a certain point of success, no becomes a rare treasure that you have to seek out, when the rest of us are still surrounded by it.

Revise Your Expectations

"I never lose. I either win or I learn."
         – Nelson Mandela

In today's society, we've developed an almost irrational fear of failure and it threatens to prevent us from developing the very qualities that help create exceptional people. Taking risks, or, conducting experiments, as I like to call it, are crucial to developing the confidence and knowledge that lead to success. As with any risk or experiment, the possibility that the result is not going to go the way that you wanted, or even needed it to at that moment, feels very real. With each risk is the possibility of collecting a puzzle piece to help solve the larger puzzles that lie ahead. It's a coordinate on the yet uncharted map of your own dreams and sense of fulfillment.

We Cannot Expect to Always Win

Imagine being stripped of everything you own, absolutely everything, including the certainty of your next meal and drink. Imagine that you have also been denied the right to attend school, have never learned how to read and lost your father to A.I.D.S. at the age of 3.

You are 9 years old. In the Ugandan slum, your lanky frame tracks behind your brother, hoping that wherever he is going, food will be there also.

What you cannot imagine is that following your brother will lead to a worn-down dilapidated church, which looks like it could collapse at any moment. In this place of worship you will find first your deliverance from hunger, and second your deliverance from your circumstances. But this is not a traditional mission, or a walk of faith through lessons on religion. Here, you will learn how to play chess.

In this story, "you" are the incredible Phiona Mutesi, the proclaimed *Queen of Katwe*, and this is how she discovered what would lead her to earning the title of Women Candidate Master from the World Chess Federation at age 16— a mere seven years from the time she picked up her first chess piece, and only two years after she had just begun learning to read and write. And while the title sounds impressive, it is levels away from the ambition that Phiona set her sights on in 2006, to become a Grandmaster. For a girl whose first words to her mother following an incredible sweep in the African International Children's chess Tournament were, "do we have enough food for breakfast?" normally, this would be easily labeled as impossible.[55]

Living through life's harshest circumstances, yet powered and empowered by a laser-like focus on something greater, has turned Phiona into a determined champion. Known for her reputation as an aggressive player, her experience representing Uganda at the 2010 Chess Olympiad in Khanty-Mansiysk, Russia was depicted in the Walt Disney film, *The Queen of Katwe*. In it, a young and overwhelmed Phiona was rattled following a loss to Taiwan's Elaine Lin Yu-Tong. The young girl who so confidently says to her coach, "I have to lose, so I can learn how to win" uncharacteristically ran from the Olympic playing area and returned to her hotel room, unaccompanied through an unfamiliar land, to collapse in a comfortless deluge of tears.

According to the account of Tim Crothers, who published the original story that brought Phiona's accomplishments to mass attention, Phiona was inconsolable, not because she had lost, but because she had lost when she believed that she should have and could have won. In a later round of that same competition, Phiona's loss to a more skilled competitor was greeted with a hopeful outlook. Energized by the lessons of competition, she told her coach, Robert Katende, "Coach, I will be a grandmaster someday."[56]

You would think, that for someone facing so much opposition, so many hurdles—not just to dreams, but life itself, the added sting of failure and loss could quench the fire of the spirit. But not for Phiona. For her, the sting of loss inspired and pushed her to go harder, to work hard, and try harder. She doesn't expect to always win—not in life and not in front of the chessboard—but losing so much and so often has truly taught her *how* to lose, so that she *can* win.

The True Compass of Success

People who are successful may have a variety of skills, but we can be sure that they are great at one thing in particular: surmounting setbacks and obstacles. Each person's path to success, their vision and dream, is different. The steps range widely and the ideas that lead to new possibilities are informed by the broadest spectrum of experiences. Ideas are not personal – one person's bright idea is another person's blunder. We treat ideas as sacred, and to a certain extent, they are. But *the true value of an idea is in its execution* and in overcoming obstacles during that process. The magic of success stories lies within those details. It is about the inner journey, the superhuman measure of determination and resilience. It is about an ability to Regroup, to refuse to accept a period at the end of the sentence they know they can continue to write.

The next time you encounter someone that you consider a success, instead of asking "how did you do it" or "do you have any advice," I challenge you to create your own powerful instruction by asking one or more of the below questions directly:

In the biggest setbacks that you've faced, did it trigger negative self-talk? If so, what did you do to combat it? If not, how did your mind become conditioned to avoid it?

How did you find resources when time or money was scarce?

When you first started out on your journey, what did you believe was impossible but turned out that it was not? How do you think about the "impossible" now? Do you still believe in the concept of impossible? If not, what do you believe and how do you look at it?

When you came up against an obstacle, how did you create options and what criteria did you use to select your next path?

What did you do to manage the negative emotions that come along the way with setbacks?

What motivated you through all of the ups and downs of your journey?

What were the biggest pitfalls or dangers, personally or otherwise, that you can recall along your path?

Getting the answers to these questions ensures that you'll cut through the irrelevant information to provide yourself with the necessary insights you need.

REGROUP NATION

In Conclusion

I believe that we all have within us the capacity for greatness. Greatness isn't uniform, or even measurable by customary means. It is the very essence of the unquenchable human spirit at its best—curious, unafraid, resilient, and hopeful for what can be made of our time on earth.

Writers are trained to focus on characters that have something to learn. We put flawed people in extreme or unusual circumstances, and then in the pages of our paper laboratory, we watch what unfolds. These flaws, we call character development; these twists of circumstance, plot. In the earliest part of my life, I certainly would have made a very poor choice of a character, as my own perfectionism confined me within the walls of others' expectations. Following the prescribed path ahead of me, there were supposed to be no twists– just a predictable existence marked by all of the trophies of success.

To this day, I cannot tell you what made me venture off course other than a dull and insistent ache that only grew in response to being ignored. It was on some random day in law school that my conscious mind finally caught up with the meaning of the aching. All it was saying was, *enough*. Enough of trying to be perfect, enough of coloring exactly in the lines, enough of doing it the "right" way with nothing to feed my soul from the inside. Enough of false safety and hoping that someone else will give me permission to jump or forgive me if I fall. *Enough*.

On that day, something was sparked within me that I've come to know as the seed of *courage*. And every day since, as long as I cultivate it, that seed continues to grow, watered and nourished by my *experiments*, the *failures* that come alongside, and the will and commitment to *Regroup*.

When I veered off track to chase my dreams and sometimes be chased by them, my life began to fall into the pages of my own fanciful laboratory and *my* character began to develop. What you've read here is some of that journey. Alongside my public and personal victories, I've also shared my shame, my disappointment, my shortcomings and my failures because it makes the plot real and complete. It is the expensive kind of honesty that we should all dare to share because it's what we could most have in common. Yes, it frightens me to be that exposed, but you are worth that risk. And my hope is that in doing so, I've somehow inspired you to find your small spark to start what will be your own plot of failing gracefully through the twists and turns of this adventure we share called life.

By now, you have powerful weapons at your disposal, should you choose to use them. These are the tools that I've learned and used on the front lines against an enemy named *impossible*. These are the keys to success that count on only two certainties in life: first, anything worth doing will present setbacks and failures along the way; and second, if you keep going, there is no way you will not succeed. Success is a journey, a fearless quest for freedom and personal fulfillment. In its own strange way, failure is the map. Without failure, a successful outcome, no matter what it was, is nothing more than a good guess.

I gave you these tools to encourage you to dream your beautiful dream. And to dream again. And again. Until that dream becomes a wish and that wish becomes a desire and that desire becomes a plan. Make your life a plot and allow your own character to develop. I've designed these tools to give you a choice—the choice to continue, or the choice to quit with your dream intact. And, I wanted you to have the choice not to make someone else's opinion of "impossible" your own.

In my highest vision, what we are starting right here, right now as you read this page in preparation to close this book, is a new part of your life and a *community*. Imagine, as I did, a place where other resilient people like you and me, come together to support each other, to protect vulnerability from shame and to share the benefit of our *experiments*, successful *and* failed, along our respective journeys to success.

I've created this place for us. It is our own Regroup Nation, and I hope that you'll join me there.

When you're ready and have decided to take that first step forward, come to RegroupNation.com, we'll be waiting for you with the light on.

Acknowledgments

The road to completion of this book, Regroup, has been its own fantastic journey. It has given me the opportunity to practice almost every aspect and element that it prescribes to be resilient and to refuse to be stopped in reaching a goal. Thank you for reading my work. What an incredible blessing to be the conduit for such a powerful message at such a time as this.

Although my name is on the cover of this book, I did not and could not have accomplished its writing on my own. So, it gives me immense joy to thank the wonderful people who supported, encouraged, sponsored, pushed, tolerated and backed me to reach this place.

Of course, I must attribute my inspiration and gifts to God, from whom all of my generous blessings flow. I cannot quantify or qualify my gratitude.

Thank you to my incredible parents, John and Shermane, who have made and continually make it their life mission to ensure that I have the opportunity to be my very best self.

Thank you to my extended family, Danielle - my sister, Myles - the best partner that a girl could dream of, and all of my incredible friends and family for the love and support that keep me shining brightly.

Thank you to my mentors – I am so fortunate to have you. Through your wisdom, patience, loyalty, guidance and unselfish investment of time and resources into my growth, I am able to walk well-prepared into the world to deliver my gifts. Craig, you are the best of the best. I thank you for always holding a light up for me to shine.

Thank you to Tim Vandehey for helping me to outline my thoughts clearly, and to editor extraordinaire Etinosa Agbonlahor for being an incredible partner in taking this manuscript to its full potential.

And last, but certainly, absolutely not least, I am extending a huge and tremendous thank you to the people who made a pledge to back me during my spectacular failure of a Kickstarter crowdfunding campaign for this book! You make my world go round. I appreciate you, each and every single one: Bernice Grant | Myles Collins | Sanyin Siang | Danielle Gray | Lori Rosario-Griffin | MeditationInMind. com | Nicole Serena Silver | Treshawn Shields | John Sealey | Shermane Sealey | Nicole Groves | Sierra Pride Home Healthcare | Liara Tamani | Crystal Zehetner | Randall Jackson | Marcus Bell | Kelli Johnson | April Carter Grant | Shelita Burke | Janice Burgess | Bill Williams | Holly Lake | Jason E. Kelly | Kevin Thibadeaux | Liliana

Grace McGee | Zak Kidd | Edward Babbage | Aaron Harrison | Eureka Gilkey | Myesha Ward | Lacey Schwartz | Kathleen Hahn | Carmen Davis Dye | Darius Monsef IV | Jennifer Jefferson | Elijah Kim | Jenny Urizar | David Nguyen | Nicole and Ric Swiner | Cheryl Inokon | Dr. Reginald and Bobby Baugh | Adia May | Charles Inokon and Andrea Martin Inokon | Kelly Shapiro | Ashley Darkenwald | Danica Wilson | Ranvir Gujral | Sharon Y. Bordeaux | Idris Manley | Helen Kathryn Sernett | Bart Decrem | Deborah Sass | Roger Drakes | LaSean Smith | Karen Vesprini | Tiffany Hall | Diahanna Nicole Baxter | Nyssa Kourakos.

To Regroup Nation, this is just the *beginning.* Let's do this!

Endnotes

1. "Beyoncé - ***Flawless ft. Chimamanda Ngozi Adichie," VEVO/YouTube video, 4:12, music video, post-ed by "beyonceVEVO," on November 24, 2014, last accessed March 9, 2017, https://www.youtube.com/watch?v=IyuUWOnS9BY.

2. "Star Search Girls Tyme with Beyonce," YouTube video, 2:45, recording of television program Star Search, posted by "Beyoncé Rockinrio" on March 28, 2013, last accessed March 9, 2017, https://www.youtube.com/watch?v=Y4ut_iGWvNs.

3. Will Anderson. "How to Run the World: The Story of How Beyoncé Seized It All." Bard Free Press, February 2013, last accessed March 9, 2017, http://bardfreepress-blog.tumblr.com/post/44083224396/how-to-run-the-world-the-story-of-how-beyonc%C3%A9.

4. "Self-Titled: Part 2. Imperfection," YouTube video, 4:35, documentary video, posted by "Beyoncé," on December 17, 2013, last accessed March 9, 2017, https://youtu.be/cIv1z6n3Xxo.

5. Beyoncé Knowles, Kelly Rowland and Michelle Williams with James Patrick Herman, Sour Survivors: The Official Autobiography of Destiny's Child (New York: HarperCollins 2002), 70.

6. Ibid, 71.

7. Michael Hall, "It's a Family Affair," Texas Monthly, April 2004, last accessed March 9, 2017, http://www.texasmonthly.com/articles/its-a-family-affair/.

8. Ibid.

9. Jessica Selinger, Shawn O'Connor, Jeremy Wong, and J. Maxwell Donelan, "Humans Can Continuously Optimize Energetic Cost During Walking," Current Biology (September 10 2015), last accessed March 9, 2017, http://www.cell.com/current-biology/fulltext/S0960-9822(15)00958-6. For other interesting articles on this topic, see the following: "Born to Be Lazy!" https://www.thenakedscientists.com/articles/interviews/born-be-lazy; and "It's My Nervous System That's Lazy!" https://www.nytimes.com/2015/09/15/science/its-my-nervous-system-thats-lazy.html?.

10. "GoPro Inc. – Market Cap Market Cap," Yahoo! Finance, last accessed March 9, 2017, http://finance.yahoo.com/quote/GPRO?p=GPRO.

11. Ryan Mac, "Five Startup Lessons from GoPro Founder and Billionaire Nick Woodman," Forbes, March 13, 2013, last accessed March 9, 2017, https://www.forbes.com/sites/ryanmac/2013/03/13/five-startup-lessons-from-gopro-founder-and-billionaire-nick-woodman/#70317cec546e.

12. Tom Foster, "The GoPro Army," Inc Magazine, Feburary 2012, last accessed March 9, 2017, http://www.inc.com/magazine/201202/the-gopro-army.html.

13. Ibid.

14. Allison Schrager, "Failed Entrepreneurs Find More Success the Second Time," Bloomberg, July 28, 2014, last accessed March 9, 2017, https://www.bloomberg.com/news/articles/2014-07-28/study-failed-entrepreneurs-find-success-the-second-time-around.

15. Kadijah Williams, quoted in "Kadijah's Journey: Skid Row to Harvard," last accessed Feb 26, 2017, http://www.oprah.com/world/khadijahs-journey-from -skid-row-to-harvard.

16. M. A. Rosanoff, "Edison in His Laboratory," Harper's, September 1932, 402-417.

17. Thomas Edison, quoted in Ibid.

18. Napoleon Hill, Think and Grow Rich, (New York: Random House 1960), 3-4.

19. Keith Petrie, Ian Fontanilla, Mark G. Thomas, Roger Booth, James W. Pennebaker, "Effect of Written Emotional Expression on Immune Function in Patients With Human Immunodeficiency Virus Infection: a randomized trial," Journal of Psychosomatic Medicine, PubMed (PMID: 15039514).

20. Stefanie P. Spera, Eric D. Buhrfeind, and James W. Pennebaker, "Expressive Writing and Coping with Job Loss," Academy of Management Journal (June 1, 1994), 722-733.

21. "Adults forget three things, a day, research finds," The Telegraph, Jul 23, 2009, last accessed March 9, 2017, http://www.telegraph.co.uk/news/uknews/5891701/Adults-forget-three-things-a-day-research-finds.html.

22. "Memory lapse – four things slip our mind every day" SWNS Blog, September 2013, last accessed March 7, 2017, http://www.swnsdigital.com/2013/09/memory-lapse/.

23. George Dvorsky, "Our Brains Deliberately Make Us Forget Things To Prevent Insanity," Gizmodo, March 14, 2014, last accessed March 9, 2017, http://io9.gizmodo.com/our-brains-deliberately-make-us-forget-things-to-preve-1543846375.

24. Hampus Jakobsson. "How We Debriefed When Our Startup Folded," Medium.com Blog, July 4, 2016, last accessed March 9, 2017, https://hajak.se/how-we-debriefed-when-our-startup-folded-80e9514491af#.mgg1mynjo.

25. Ibid.

26. Philip Ullrich and Susan K Lutgendorf, "Journaling About Stressful Events: Effects of Cognitive Processing and Emotional Expreession," Annals of Behavioral Medicine (2002), Vol. 24, No. 3.

27. Marla Tabaka, "Make failure good for you," Inc. Magazine, July 9, 2012, last accessed March 9, 2017, http://www.inc.com/marla-tabaka/fail-good-to-succeed.html.

28. "Forbes Global 500," Forbes Magazine, last accessed February 26, 2017, http://beta.fortune.com/global500/.

29. "Toyota Production System," Wikipedia, last accessed February 26, 2017, https://en.wikipedia.org/wiki/Toyota_Production_System.

30. "5 Whys," Wikipedia, last accessed February 26, 2017, https://en.wikipedia.org/wiki/5_Whys.

31. Ibid.

32. Robert Frank, "Billionaire Sara Blakely says secret to success is failure." CNBC, October 13, 2013, last accessed March 9, 2017, http://www.cnbc.com/2013/10/16/billionaire-sara-blakely-says-secret-to-success-is-failure.html.

33. Matthew Belvedere, "'My own butt' Spanx inspiration: Billionaire Inventor," CNBC, October 16, 2013, last accessed March 9, 2017, http://www.cnbc.com/2013/10/16/my-own-butt-spanx-inspriation-billionaire-inventor.html.

34. W.J. Hennigan, "Forbes: Spanx inventor is youngest self-made female billionaire," Los Angeles Times, March 9, 2012, last accessed March 9, 2017, http://articles.latimes.com/2012/mar/09/business/la-fi-spanx-billionaire-20120309.

35. Wendy Mead, W. Sara Blakely Biography, Bio., last updated March 14, 2016, last accessed March 9,

2017, http://www.biography.com/people/sara-blakely-031416.

36. Sara Blakely, quoted in Jill Becker, "Shaping Sara Blakely: Meet the Billionaire Founder of Spanx," Success, December 7, 2015, last accessed March 9, 2017, http://www.success.com/article/shaping-sara-blakely-meet-the-billionaire-founder-of-spanx.

37. Ibid.

38. Jill Becker, "21 Bits of Wit and Wisdom from the Woman Behind the Billion-Dollar Brand," Success, December 8, 2015, last accessed March 9, 2017, http://www.success.com/article/21-bits-of-wit-and-wisdom-from-the-woman-behind-the-billion-dollar-brand.

39. Angela Duckworth, Grit, (New York: Scribner/Simon & Schuster 2016), 241.

40. Melissa Dahl, "How Neuroscientists Explain the Mind-Clearing Magic of Running," New York Magazine, April 16, 2016, last accessed March 9, 2017, http://nymag.com/scienceofus/2016/04/why-does-running-help-clear-your-mind.html.

41. Emily E. Bernstein and Richard McNally, "Acute aerobic exercise helps over come emotional regulation deficits," Journal of Cognition and Emotion, April 4, 2016, last accessed March 9, 2017, (2016, Apr 4), doi: 10.1080/02699931.2016.1168284.

42. Doc Searls (David Searls), "DIY Radio with PODcasting," Doc Searls IT Garage Blog, archive of September 28, 2004 post, last accessed March 9, 2017, https://web.archive.org/web/20080321031647/http://www.itgarage.com/node/462.

43. "History of Podcasting." Wikipedia, last accessed February 26, 2017, https://en.wikipedia.org/wiki/History_of_podcasting.

44. Nicholas Carlson, "How Twitter Was Founded," Business Insider, April 13, 2011, last accessed March 9, 2017, http://www.businessinsider.com/how-twitter-was-founded-2011-4.

45. "Fanzy," AngelList, last accessed March 9, 2017, https://angel.co/fanzy.

46. Jeff Marois, interview with the author, November 2016.

47. "Announcing the 2016 Sprudgie Awards Finalists," December 14, 2016, last accessed March 9, 2017, http://sprudge.com/announcing-2016-sprudgie-awards-finalists-113429.html.

48. Mary Papenfuss, "Mom and Kids Build House, One YouTube Video at a Time," January 17, 2017, last accessed March 9, 2017, http://www.huffingtonpost.com/entry/mom-and-kids-build-house-one-youtube-tutorial-video-at-a-time_us_5878700ae4b09281d0ea4989.

49. Randall Stephenson, quoted in Quentin Hardy, "Gearing Up For the Cloud, AT&T Tells Its Workers: Adapt, Or Else," New York Times, February 13, 2016, last accessed March 9, 2017, https://www.nytimes.com/2016/02/14/technology/gearing-up-for-the-cloud-att-tells-its-workers-adapt-or-else.html.

50. Matthew Narvin, "He Made a Secret Album in an Apple Store," The Daily Beast, July 14, 2015, last accessed March 9, 2017, http://www.thedailybeast.com/articles/2015/07/05/he-made-a-secret-album-in-an-apple-store.html.

51. Thomas Edison, statement in a press conference (1929), quoted in James D. Newton, Uncommon Friends: Life with Thomas Edison, Henry Ford, Harvey Firestone, Alexis Carrel & Charles Lindbergh (Boston: Mariner Books 1989), 24.

52. Sophia Amoruso, "A decade above the influence. Onward babies. I love you.," Twitter, No-

vember 9, 2016, last accessed March 9, 2017, https://twitter.com/sophiaamoruso/status/796558139503976448?lang=en.

53. Sophia Amoruso, quoted in Lauren Sherman, "Nasty Gal: What Went Wrong?," Business of Fashion. November 15, 2016, last accessed March 9, 2017, https://www.businessoffashion.com/articles/intelligence/nasty-gal-what-went-wrong.

54. Eliza Brooke, "Nasty Gal Just Filed for Bankruptcy. How Did it Get Here?," Racked, November 10, 2016, last accessed March, 9, 2017, http://www.racked.com/2016/11/10/13587674/nasty-gal-bankruptcy

55. Tim Crothers, "Game of Her Life," ESPN Magazine, April 12, 2013, last accessed March 9, 2017, http://www.espn.com/espn/news/story?page=Mag15gameofherlife.

56. Ibid.

Made in the USA
Middletown, DE
05 May 2018